FAST PATCH

KIDS' QUILTS

FAST PATCH

KIDS' QUILTS

Anita Hallock

Betsy Hallock Heath

krause
publications

Published by Krause Publications, Iola, Wisconsin

Designed by Ayers/Johanek Publication Design, Inc.
The photograph on page 70 was taken by Blink Ink in Pittsburgh, PA.
The photographs on pages 2, 4, 5, 9, 18, 25, and 93 were taken
by Dave Heath.
All other photographs were taken by Walt Biddle, many at Wyatt
Elementary School. We appreciate the cooperation of Kathy Biddle,
teacher.
Illustrations by Anita Hallock

Manufactured in the United States of America

Library of Congress Cataloging-in-Publication Data

Hallock, Anita
  Fast Patch kids' quilts:dozens of designs to make for and with
  kids/Anita hallock, Betsy Hallock Heath.
      p. cm.
    Includes index.
    ISBN 0-8019-8741-5 (pbk)
    1. Patchwork—Patterns. 2. Strip quilting—Patterns.
  3. Children's quilts. I. Heath, Betsy Hallock. II. Title.
  TT835.H3333 1996
  746.46'041—dc20   96-23969
                                                   CIP

  3 4 5 6 7 8 9 0   5 4 3 2 1 0 9

To Kelly, David, Joseph, and Hannah

CONTENTS

A Note from Anita   ix

CHAPTER ONE
Kids and Quilts   1

Why We Make Quilts for Kids   1

Loved for a Long Time?   2

If It Won't Be Pampered, Make It Tough   3

Look for the 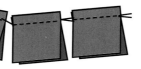 Smiling Patch   3

CHAPTER TWO
Quiltmaking Materials and Techniques   5

Supplies   5

Fabric   6

Colors and Prints to Use for Kids' Quilts   7

Basic Sewing and Pressing   9

Strip-Piecing or Traditional Piecing?   9

Assembling the Quilt   11

Quilting or Tying?   12

Finishing the Quilt   14

CHAPTER THREE
Playing with Blocks   17

Some Simple Block Arrangements   18

Setting Blocks on Point   19

A Surprise Variation—The Storybook Quilt   21

Nine Patch Storybook Quilt   22

Checkerboard Storybook Quilt   23

Twin Storybook Quilt   24

Creative Arrangements   25

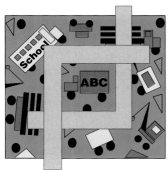

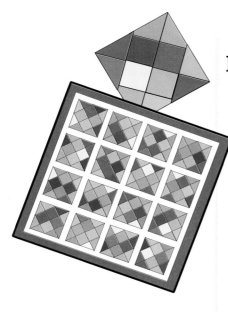

CHAPTER FOUR
Dancing Squares   26
Checkerboard Quilts   26
Two-Color Checkerboard Quilt   27
Flannel Scrap Quilt   28
Jiffy Quilt   28
Grandma's Secret   30
Dancing Squares   32
Dancing Squares Quilt   32

CHAPTER FIVE
Magic Triangles   34
Strip-Piecing Triangles   34
Success with Magic Triangles   38
Betsy's Boats   40
Betsy's Boat Blocks Assembly-Line Style   42
8 More Sailboat Blocks   44
Creative Ideas   45

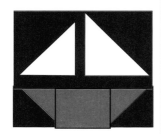

CHAPTER SIX
Nine Patch Nature Blocks   46
General Instructions for Nature Blocks   47
16 Butterfly Blocks   48
16 Tulip Blocks   49
8 Songbird Blocks   50
8 Maple Leaf Blocks   51
8 Sawtooth Flower Blocks   52

8 Simplified Flower Blocks   53

8 Butterfly Fish Blocks   54

8 Simple Fish Blocks   55

8 Angel Fish Blocks   56

Using the Leftovers: 8 Fish-in-a-Flash   57

Standard 15-Block Nature Quilt   58

Other Settings and Borders   59

Other Creative Ideas   61

CHAPTER SEVEN

The Playroom Quilt   64

Overview of the Toy Blocks   65

Fabric and Embellishments   66

Getting Organized   67

Cutting the Pieces   67

How to Assemble and Embellish the Blocks 70

Complete the Quilt Top   74

More Ideas   75

Appendix   91

A Coordinated Nursery Set   91

Bumper Pad   91

Dust Ruffle for a Crib   92

Templates for Making
   Nine Patch Nature Blocks   94

Special Things to Order   96

Glossary   97

Index   98

About the Authors   102

A NOTE FROM ANITA

Writers usually go through a series of working titles. One of mine was *Fast Patch: The Next Generation*, not only because the quilts are for children (in fact, your child could help make many of them) but also because there is new generation of ideas for strip-piecing triangles. The method I introduced in *Fast Patch: A Treasury of Strip Quilt Projects* and *Scrap Quilts Using Fast Patch* is featured, along with an alternate method that puts the bias in the "correct" position. My original title would also apply to the next generation, who helped *write* the book. My daughter Betsy has been making quilts for her children, for gifts, and to sell at craft shows since 1989.

Since I actually wrote the text, that's who "I" refers to. Betsy made samples and reviewed all the ideas. From her production quiltmaking, she knows how to make quilts quickly and knows what people like to buy for children. And she knows what children themselves like, since she has four of them: Kelly, age 8; David, age 6; Joseph, age 4; and Hannah, age 1 (as we went to press in 1996).

I want to thank my husband, George, who has been a great help at shows and retreats. I know he longs for bygone days when wives didn't have computers and didn't play with fabric until the laundry, cooking, and housecleaning were done. He's become very helpful with two of those chores and very tolerant of leftovers.

And I thank my son-in-law Dave, who patiently supports Betsy in all her projects.

Betsy and I hope you—and your Favorite Little People—enjoy this book.

ANITA HALLOCK
Springfield, Oregon
1996

CHAPTER ONE

Kids and Quilts

WHY WE MAKE QUILTS FOR KIDS

Although quilts keep youngsters warm, we make quilts mostly to show our love. We think fondly about our Favorite Little Person (FLP) as we sew. If we're lucky, the youngster will think fondly about who made the quilt—but that may come 20 years from now.

Some quilts might go to children we never meet. They might be contributed to babies born with AIDS, stashed in police cruisers to comfort children snatched from violent homes or crime scenes, or sent to families left homeless by disasters. They show we care about their heartaches, even if we personally can't be out there fighting all the nasty and dangerous things going on in the world.

Some of these projects might not go to any child, period. You might make such a beautiful quilt that you'll decide to keep it as a wallhanging and not let your Favorite Little Person near it until he or she becomes a teenager. That's okay. Substitute a quick cuddly quilt and leave the masterpiece hanging on the wall, where it can still be a precious gift to the child—an example of how a person can ponder, dream, struggle, learn, and work to turn a pile of fabric into something unique and beautiful. It's also an example of how fine handiwork should be cherished.

One-year-old Hannah loves this cozy Flannel Scrap Quilt made by her mother, Betsy. Directions for this quilt are in Chapter 4.

LOVED FOR A LONG TIME?

One title I considered for this book was *Loved for a Long Time*. It had a great sound, but I decided that it might be misleading. If it's loved too thoroughly, a quilt won't last a long time—unless it's made of durable fabric. But quiltmakers prefer to work with lightweight cotton, which will fade and wear out with everyday use.

A child isn't born with the instinct to take care of possessions, especially those as delicate as quilts. He must be taught, and you can give some basic instructions with a special gift tag.

Here are some quilt care tags you can customize to fit the quilt and the family in your life. Blank out the things you don't want (if your quilt isn't 100% cotton, for example), cut and paste the art, and add new ideas, if you want. Here are four versions.

The first is an all-purpose tag. You could substitute your own art for the sailboats.

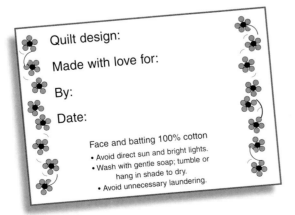

Here's another all-purpose tag. This one has a floral border.

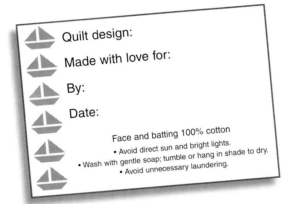

This tag is for a wallhanging. (Be sure to add the hanging sleeve to your quilt if you use this tag.)

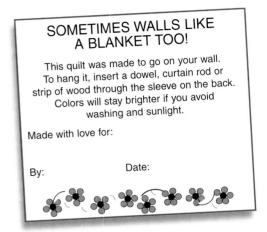

If the quilt is durable or if you don't want to make it seem so precious that no one can touch it, use this tag. Instead of saying, "Take good care of it," it says, "I made it because I care about you." If the quilt will go to a child you don't know, sign the tag with only your first name, or use the bunny picture with the "secret friend" tag.

A hug for you from a secret friend.

The quilt still won't last forever, so get a good photograph of it (with the child, if possible) for your own fond memories, then let it go. Try not to be shocked if you see the quilt in tatters later because it was loved too rambunctiously; it served its purpose.

IF IT WON'T BE PAMPERED, MAKE IT TOUGH

If you make quilts for homeless children, think it through. A delicate cotton quilt would probably be loved, all right, especially by a child who hasn't much else to call his own. But what happens when the quilt starts looking shabby? That could happen fast when someone lives in a car or crowded shelter. The quilt might be dragged around a campground, with other children and dogs grabbing at it. If there are only enough coins for one batch of laundry, it might be washed with socks, jeans, and everything else and then draped over a fence or the hood of the car to dry in the sun. Parents trying to bring order and beauty back into their lives might not appreciate their child being attached to a shabby quilt. Do everyone a favor and make the quilt from poplin.

Instead of taking days or weeks on an elaborate quilt for one child, make durable, colorful quilts for a half-dozen children by choosing easy designs like these:

✦ Nine Patch Blocks alternating with plain blocks (page 18)
✦ Flannel Scrap Quilt (page 28)
✦ Jiffy Quilt (pages 28–29)
✦ Dancing Squares Quilt (page 32)
✦ Grandma's Secret (page 30)

Or make the What's-on-Hand Quilt (page 25) from recycled blue jeans. Include pockets, and tuck a surprise in each—maybe a little car, a doll, a quarter, a motel-size bottle of hand lotion or shampoo, or a box of crayons. A youngster rescued from disaster may have left all his or her treasures behind.

LOOK FOR THE SMILING PATCH

If your Favorite Little Person (FLP) wanders by and asks to help, switch gears immediately and get him or her involved. (If you are working on your own special quilt, have a children's project ready to substitute.) Doing a project with a little person will create some of the best memories you can have. Get someone to hover in the background with a camera or camcorder, if possible. Computers, TV, sports, and divided families make life for many children much different from the way it was

♥ ♥ ♥
We loved this poem by Nancy Ridell and wanted to share it with you.*

IT'S YOUR QUILT

It's OK if you sit on your quilt.
It's OK if your bottle gets spilt,
If you swallow some air
And you burp, don't despair;
It's OK if you spit on your quilt.

There are scraps old and new on your quilt,
Put together for you on your quilt.
If your gums feel numb
'Cause your teeth haven't come,
It's OK if you chew on your quilt.

We expect you to lie on your quilt.
If you hurt, you may cry on your quilt.
On a cold rainy night,
Don't you fret; you're all right;
You'll be snug, warm and dry on your quilt.

*Reprinted by permission of the author. First printed in *Quilter's Newsletter Magazine*, No. 279 (Jan.–Feb. 1996), p. 44.

Joseph Heath (age four) and his brother, David (age six), help design their Storybook Quilts. Note that they did not follow the "rules" for these quilts (given in Chapter 3)— that's okay though, because when it comes to design, your Favorite Little People are always right!

when we were young. Moments when you, the little person, the supplies, the interest, and the time are all together at once might not come very often. Trust me.

Some steps in most projects can be done by a child. Look for the smiling patch in the margin as a signal that your FLP might be able to help at that stage. Use the smiling patch as a general guide. Some kids are too young for any involvement, and some might be able to make the whole quilt by themselves.

When your blocks are spread out on the floor in an overall arrangement, it's great to have a child hand you the blocks and return them to their spots. It keeps the block arrangement intact and saves you lots of getting up and down from the sewing machine.

Most kids can make choices about how to arrange colors or blocks. As a general rule, if a little person makes a thoughtful choice about such matters, the decision is final. Sometime in the future, she might decide for herself the arrangement isn't perfect, but she won't have an unpleasant memory of you correcting her choice. You'll have a chance to make masterpiece quilts later, and so will she, but childhood comes only once. ★

CHAPTER TWO

Quiltmaking Materials and Techniques

This chapter covers supplies to have on hand, as well as techniques you'll need to know to make the quilt blocks shown in this book. Information on fabric and color choices are also provided to help you get the most out of your quilting experience.

Betsy helps seven-year-old Kelly cut with a rotary cutter. Never let youngsters use these razor-sharp tools alone.

SUPPLIES

You don't need a lot of tools to make great quilts. Here we discuss cutting tools, sewing machines, needles, and threads.

ROTARY CUTTING TOOLS

Most quiltmakers now use rotary cutters since they can cut through many layers, and are faster and more accurate than scissors.

✦ **Rotary cutter.** Choose a rotary cutter with a large blade. For safety, use one with a cover that must be deliberately pushed back, not one that automatically retracts when you cut. Cutters are extremely sharp, so never set the cutter down, even for an instant, without snapping the cover in place—especially if there are children around.

✦ *Cutting mat.* Buy the largest cutting mat size you can afford and have room for. A 24" × 36" mat is good if you can afford only one, but it's really handy to have a smaller mat also.

✦ *Ruler.* Get a quilter's 6" × 24" ruler with ⅛" marks and 45° angle lines. These rulers are transparent so you can line up fabric with the measurement lines and are thick so you can cut against them without having the blade jump the edge. Transparent square grids (9", 12", 15", or 18") are needed for some projects, especially those using the Two-Square method for triangles.

Trim, Move, Cut, Cut

Here's how to cut fabric strips using your rotary cutter and ruler. Since many projects use 4" strips, use that width for your practice cuts.

1 Trim. First stack or fold over layers of fabric, lining up one or more edges. Next place the quilter's ruler over the fabric just inside the aligned edges. Spread out one hand to hold the ruler so it doesn't slip. With your other hand, hold the cutter firmly against the ruler and trim off the edges of the fabric.

2 Move. Walk around the table or turn the mat so you can continue to cut at a natural angle. Never try to cut with the wrong hand or cross one hand over the other when using the rotary cutter. Move the ruler over so that the edge of the fabric is lined up with the 4" mark on the ruler.

3 Cut. Holding the ruler firmly, cut through all the layers of the fabric.

4 Cut. You can continue to cut as many strips as you need without changing your position. Just move the ruler over 4" each time.

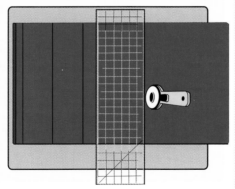

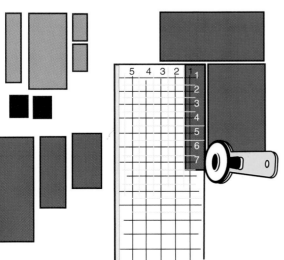

USE YOUR RULER INSTEAD OF TEMPLATES.

We usually strip-piece quilts instead of using the small pieces of traditional piecing. For a project that can't be strip-pieced, we still don't make templates. We just cut out the shapes with the rotary cutter and ruler. See Chapter 7 for many examples of using your ruler in this way.

SEWING SUPPLIES

Here are the basic sewing supplies you'll want to have on hand.

Sewing Machine

All the projects in this book are machine pieced. Note that you don't need an expensive, high-tech machine; you can make all the quilts in this book with any machine that will sew a straight line. Some machines are better than others for free-motion machine quilting, however, so check that quality if you're in the market for a new model.

If a child is learning to sew, it's nice to have a machine whose speed can be controlled. It's frustrating and scary to have the machine go too fast.

Thread

Some quilters insist on 100% cotton thread, but 100% polyester and cotton-wrapped polyester are easier to find and will work well. Use the same type of thread in the needle and bobbin, if possible. Use a neutral thread color when piecing if your quilt contains many colors of fabric. Never use cheap bargain-table threads; they make sewing more difficult and may foul up your machine. We sometimes use transparent thread or metallic thread for machine quilting.

Needles

First, be sure that you use the needles recommended by the manufacturer of your machine. Use the smallest size that is appropriate and change needles frequently. Don't use a needle until it breaks (as I used to do, wondering why I had problems with tension and skipped stitches). Use dull needles for thumbtacks—no guilt about throwing away a "good" needle that way.

FABRIC

Like most quiltmakers, we usually use 100% cotton fabrics. These fabrics come in a huge choice of colors and designs, cotton is pleasant to work with, and the finished quilt is comfortable.

But cotton isn't perfect. It is flammable; soils easily; deteriorates in sunlight; and may shrink, fade, and wrinkle. "Easy-care" cottons probably have a formaldehyde resin in them, to which some people are allergic, just as some are allergic to polyester. Prewashing removes much of the formaldehyde and repeated washing will probably remove the rest. (If a project is quilted enough, the fabric doesn't need to be permanent press.)

According to *Claire Shaeffer's Fabric Sewing*

Guide (Chilton, 1994), the best quality cotton is:

♦ *Made from long-staple cotton, such as Pima cotton.* Test the fiber length by pulling a thread out and untwisting it; if the fibers are longer than 1/2", the fabric will wear well.

♦ *Tightly woven.* Test the weave by scraping the fabric with a thumbnail; if the yarns separate easily, the fabric won't wear well. Try holding the fabric up to a light; the weave should be uniform.

♦ *Soft when purchased, because it doesn't have heavy sizing.* Test the fabric by holding it up to a light and seeing if there is sizing between the threads. Try rubbing the fabric briskly; if it then feels softer and your hands feel powdery, the fabric has too much sizing.

Here are some other things to keep in mind:

♦ The fabric will probably be printed off grain a little, and if it has a permanent press finish, it probably can't be straightened.

♦ Most of the projects call for 44"-wide fabric; if yours is only 42" wide, you shouldn't have any problems. But please read through the directions before you begin the quilt.

♦ Wash all new fabric, after clipping a small triangle off each corner to help prevent raveling. If the wash water is colored, wash and dry the fabric again. Place a square of white cotton in the same wash batch to help you monitor color bleeding.

♦ Don't use a fabric if the colors continue to bleed after two or three wash cycles. I once complimented a mother on her cute baby girl, only to find out it was a baby boy—the pink quilt around him had started out as a red and white one. (Today's children aren't supposed to be restricted by gender stereotypes, but the mom looked annoyed.)

DURABLE FABRICS

Use durable fabrics (and simple patchwork blocks) for camp quilts or quilts for homeless children. Durable cottons include the following:

♦ *Broadcloth.* Fine cross-rib fabric; very durable.

♦ *Chino.* Durable, medium-weight twill-weave fabric, with a slight sheen on one side.

♦ *Percale.* Made from long fibers.

♦ *Flannel.* Napped on one or both sides; it's warm and cozy.

♦ *Poplin.* Lightweight, firm, cross-rib fabric; if poor quality, it will slip at the seams.

♦ *Twill, including denim.* Most durable weave; it's heavy and the colors are limited.

Betsy's Ocean Quilt (top) has several fish swimming one way and smaller fish in the distance swimming the other way. Notice the appliquéd sea life near the bottom of the quilt. Anita's Spring Garden Quilt (bottom) uses four Songbird and four Butterfly blocks at the top. The center suggests a wrought-iron fence, and there are Simplified Sawtooth Flowers near the bottom. The stamens and pistils were embroidered using metallic threads. These blocks can all be found in Chapter 6.

Betsy has found that people promptly snatch up any flannel baby quilts she has for sale. Use flannel for the back of the quilt or for very simple designs on the front. These days, printed flannels are popular, so there's a huge selection, which may not be true in years to come.

Use twills only for quilts with simple designs and those that might be taken outdoors. If you want to use denim, cut up old jeans, which have already shrunk, faded, and softened.

Also try indestructible double-knit polyester. But don't use a light color since polyester stains badly, and avoid the types that snag. Cut up some bright polyester pants from Goodwill perhaps.

COLORS AND PRINTS TO USE FOR KIDS' QUILTS

If you know which bedroom the quilt will be used in, and that room has a specific color scheme, by all means choose colors to match. If the youngster you're making the quilt for is nearby, ask his or her opinion on colors and fabrics. Otherwise, choose colors that please kids in general or colors that you enjoy working with.

Although you may have to choose all your fabric ahead of time when you're taking a class, there's no need to do this if you're sewing at home and have a lot of fabrics to choose from. When the quilt top is partly done, it's easy to lay

This quilt was made by Renee Sullivan of Springfield, Oregon. It is a good example of the use of colors from Anita's book Fast Patch: A Treasury of Strip Quilt Projects (see the Appendix).

out sections and see what colors you need to add next.

CHOOSING COLORS

I find my attention wanders when I try to study color schemes. Unless you make a living as a designer or do prepress work for four-color printing, I think you can work mostly by intuition. There are a few basic rules that have served us well. Any of these rules can be ignored, if the colors you select please you and the youngster.

You can't go wrong with bright colors for the kids themselves, although you can disappoint parents if the quilt's colors clash with the bedroom's colors. If the colors are high contrast (red, yellow, and blue, for example), don't use them in equal amounts. Have one of the colors dominate, reinforcing it by using some closely related colors; use less of the contrasting colors. When the dyes are subdued or enhanced by being mixed with other colors, you get what we call "mixed" colors. Most of our favorite colors for adult quilts are in this category—forest greens, mossy greens, cranberry, and mauve, for example. Use mixed colors with each other, but maybe not with bright colors. (Bright red is often a nice accent with subtle shades of greens and blues, however.) Avoid drab colors for kids' quilts, except as neutrals to tone down bright colors.

Avoid black (except for wallhangings) since it fades to a drab color after several washings. Navy blue might work just as well as a dark accent, and it will age to a more pleasant color.

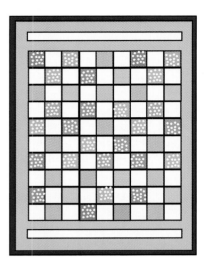

Use pastels mostly for infant quilts, since kids like brighter colors and pastels can become quite colorless after a few launderings. Also use pastels instead of pure white, since they won't show the dirt as much.

Warm and Cool Colors

Whether bright or mixed, drab or pastel, colors come in two families: the warm colors are the reds, red-violets, oranges, yellows, browns, and beiges. The cool colors include the blues, most greens and purples, and the grays.

Create a quilt with mostly warm colors, using cool colors for accent, or create a quilt with mostly cool colors, using warm colors for accent.

SOLIDS, PRINTS, PLAIDS, OR STRIPES?

For most designs, use solid fabric or small or medium low-contrast prints, especially for triangles. Plaids, stripes, and large prints can be used for borders and squares. Large prints can be used for backing, for picture blocks in the Storybook Quilts, and as a central panel to put an interesting pieced border around.

We love scrap quilts for children because they have such a homey, old-fashioned look. They invite you to use them, not put them away in a chest. And your Favorite Little Person will enjoy studying the many different fabrics over the months. A child who is bedridden would especially appreciate a great variety of interesting fabrics to look at. Most of the blocks in the first half of the book would look good made with scrap fabrics.

You don't have to have a big stash of fabric to make scrap quilts. You can buy "fat quarters" (pieces that measure 18"×22") at most fabric stores. If you have friends who sew, you can usually beg, borrow, or trade fabrics, especially since you'll need such small amounts.

BASIC SEWING AND PRESSING

Use these basic quiltmaking requirements and techniques:

✦ **Stitch Length.** Set your machine to stitch about 12 stitches to the inch. A child who's helping can use larger stitches, because he or she might have to pick out seams.

✦ **Seam Width.** For quiltmaking, use 1/4" seams as a rule. You can use wider seams for the projects in the first half of the book if the quilt will get hard use, if you're using fabrics that fray, or if a child is doing the sewing.

✦ **Chaining Pieces.** When making a quilt, you'll often need to sew a whole bunch of identical units, one after another. To save time, don't remove your work from the machine after you finish a seam. Just leave pieces chained together, and clip the threads when you are done with a whole series of seams. If your machine tends to come unthreaded easily, end the chain with a piece of scrap fabric (a "thread catcher"). Leave the scrap under the presser foot until you are ready to start sewing again.

✦ **Pressing.** As a general rule, press a seam before crossing it with seams going the other direction. Press both seams to one side—usually toward the darker fabric—or press in the direction that creates less bulky seams. If you press different panels in opposite directions, the seams will butt up against each other nicely when you sew the panels together. Use spray-on fabric finish or sizing to give the fabric more body and stability.

This Sawtooth Flower Quilt, pieced by Betsy, has been spread out and layered and is ready for quilting. Her daughter Kelly (age seven) is cutting off the excess batting.

STRIP-PIECING OR TRADITIONAL PIECING?

Except for the quilt in Chapter 7, the projects in this book are strip-pieced, since that method is usually fast and interesting. The Jiffy Quilt (page 28) is very easy, even for children learning to sew. Strip-piecing *triangles* requires learning new ideas, but it's well worth it.

If you want to socialize with your helper instead of learning new strip-piecing ideas, you can rely on traditional piecing methods, cutting out the needed squares or triangles with your ruler. In the Appendix, you'll find template patterns for making the Nature blocks.

We hope you and your Favorite Little Person create wonderful memories during the hours you spend cutting pieces and sewing them together to make quilt blocks. But be aware that at any moment the project could be left for you to finish alone, thanks to children's short attention spans and the abrupt changes that take place in some families. Be sure you'll enjoy the process even without the company of your FLP.

The only block in this book that I personally would make with templates is the Doll block shown in Chapter 7.

HOW TO STRIP-PIECE NINE PATCH BLOCKS

Basic strip-piecing of squares is very easy. Try it first with the good old Nine Patch block. Tell your FLP that a hundred years ago, children would learn to sew by hand-stitching the squares together to make this very block.

You can make three blocks from just two strips of fabric. Choose a dark fabric and a light fabric.

1 Cut one light and one dark strip, each 2½"×44".

2 Cut off one 8" length from the dark strip and two 8" lengths from the light strip.

Sew the strips together like this:

3 Cut two 16" lengths from the dark strip and one 16" length from the light strip.

Sew them together like this:

4 Press the seam allowances toward the dark fabric in both panels.

5 Cut cross-sections from both panels, making them the same width as the original strips (2½" in this case).

6 Assemble the pieces into Nine Patch blocks, as shown.

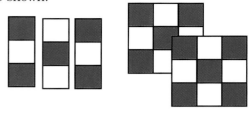

See why it's handy to have all the seams pressed toward the dark fabric? The seams can be lined up neatly without a lot of bulk.

HOW TO STRIP-PIECE A CHECKERBOARD

The Nine Patch blocks had an *odd* number of squares, so you had to cut sections from two different panels to piece it. Checkerboards have an *even* number of squares and so are made from just one panel.

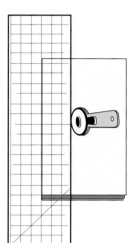

Again, choose one light and one dark fabric for this practice Checkerboard.

1 Cut two strips of dark fabric and two strips of light fabric. For this practice, make the strips 3"×13", unless you have a reason to make them a different size.

2 Sew the strips together as shown, and press the seams toward the dark fabric. Now trim off the uneven ends.

3 Cut the panel into strips going the other direction. Make these strips the same width as the original strips (3", in this case).

4 Reverse half of the strips, and sew them back together. You won't be able to press everything toward the dark now, so just press all seams in the same direction.

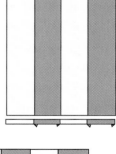

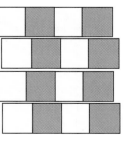

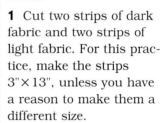

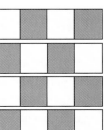

ASSEMBLING THE QUILT

Once your Nine Patch or Checkerboard blocks are made, there are so many ways to combine them that we put that information in a separate chapter. These two strip-pieced blocks are featured in the quilt top arrangements shown in Chapter 3.

BORDERS

Although you could just bind the patched edges of the quilt blocks, borders make a quilt prettier—and larger. With three borders—2", 3", and 4", respectively, after seams—a 20"×30" quilt becomes 38"×48". Wide borders are a good way to use fabric with a large print, which you wouldn't want to cut in small pieces.

Here's our general approach for adding the borders on children's quilts:

✦ Overlap the borders rather than mitering the corners, since that's much faster.

✦ We usually use 1 1/2" to 5" borders, with no two borders being the same width.

✦ We suggest cutting the borders cross grain so you can buy just 1/3 yard or so of fabric. (If you have plenty of the fabric on hand for the borders, cut with the grain, since there's less stretch.)

✦ We usually add side borders first; then add the end borders, which must be long enough to include the width of the side borders. We do this because a 44" strip is often long enough for the sides of a quilt top but would be too short if the end borders had already been added. (Feel free to add the end borders first, if that fits your fabric better.)

✦ Use a square of a different fabric in each corner if you're a bit short of border fabric.

The following directions can be used to finish any pieced quilt top.

1 Press the quilt top and smooth it out on a table or other flat surface.

2 Measure for the side borders. Measure lengthwise through the center of the quilt top; then measure each side. Use the average of the three measurements. (If there's more than a 1" difference, you might want do some fixing. Or don't bother—a handmade quilt often is not a perfect rectangle.)

3 Cut side borders. Pin the strips in a few places and sew. Press the seams.

4 Measure for the top and bottom borders. Again, measure each end and through the center, taking the average of the three measurements.

5 Cut the top and bottom borders. Pin the strips in place and sew. Press the seams.

Continue adding borders to make the quilt as large as you wish.

BATTING

Before you can quilt, you need to layer the top with batting and backing fabric. A whole chapter could be written on the different battings available today. You will find your favorite batt only through trial and error. We usually use a 4- or 6-ounce polyester batt for tied quilts. For hand or machine quilting, we use a low-loft cotton batt, since it's pleasant to work with and the layers don't slip around as much.

You might consider lining a quilt that is made from a heavy fabric with acrylic pile. In this case, no batting would be needed. The pile is warm and cozy and lasts almost forever, making it a good choice for quilts that might go to a shelter for the homeless.

Cut the batting at least 2" larger than the quilt top in each direction. If the batt has been tightly packaged, spread it out flat and let it sit overnight before cutting it.

If you want to make four baby quilts, save money by buying a queen-size batting (90"×108") and dividing it into four sections, each 45"×54". Or make two baby quilts (each 42"×58") and one twin-size quilt (48"×75" or longer) from the one queen-size batt.

BACKING

Use a colorful children's print on the back of the quilt, unless you are doing elaborate quilting you want to show off against a solid fabric. Cut the backing a little larger than the batting.

Remember, the final quilt will be slightly smaller than the dimensions of the quilt back, because you'll need to trim things up and because the quilt will shrink a bit when quilted, especially if it's machine quilted.

It's quite common to piece the back of the quilt instead of using a single fabric. See the photograph on page 12 for an example. This is

BACKING YARDAGE FOR FAST-PATCH KIDS' QUILTS

Type of Quilt	Size before Layering	Amount to Buy
Small infant quilt	33 × 41"	1 yard
Crib quilt	41 × 50"	1 1/2 yards
Child's quilt	41 × 57"	1 2/3 yards
Bunk or twin bed throw	41 × 68"	2 yards
Twin-size bedspread	51 × 85"	3 yards*

Cut fabric in half, remove the selvages, and sew it end to end.

actually the *back* of a Jiffy Quilt. If you don't have enough of the fabric you want to use for the backing, remember that you can extend it by adding other fabrics. Use some sort of embellishment (such as a strip of contrasting fabric between solid panels) to make it look as if it were an artistic decision instead of a matter of practicality. You might even want to try piecing big angular panels of fabric.

Anita decorated the back of this Jiffy Quilt with scraps left over from piecing the front. The edges were finished with the Quick-Turn method, and the quilt was machine quilted with gentle curves.

Plan ahead. If you can decide how you'll quilt your project, you can make the seams on the backing go in a different direction from the quilting design.

LAYERING THE QUILT

Follow these steps for layering your quilt top, batt, and backing.

1 Press the quilt top and backing fabric.

2 Cut the batting (which you have "lofted" by letting it lie flat overnight) 2" larger than the quilt top, and cut the backing fabric to the same size or a little larger.

3 Spread the backing fabric out, wrong side up. If you're making a large quilt, you'll need to hold the backing fabric taut somehow. (Pin it to a quilting frame, tape it to a table or floor with masking tape, clip it to a table with large bulldog clips, etc.) If you're making a small quilt, just spread it our on any flat surface.

4 Spread out the batting on top of the backing, being careful not to stretch it.

5 Spread out the quilt top on top of the batting, right side up.

QUILTING OR TYING?

There are three basic ways to attach the quilt top, batting, and backing together: hand quilting, tying, and machine quilting.

If you are making a quilt you hope will be an heirloom, by all means hand quilt it, if you enjoy the process. There are several good books on the market in which you can find detailed instructions for hand quilting. For the projects in this book we recommend tying. Tying is easy, friendly, and invites children to get involved. Machine quilting can be just as fast as tying and usually makes the quilt more durable. You can combine techniques as well. For example you could tie the quilt top center, but machine quilt the borders in place. If your areas of machine quilting are inconspicuous, you might want to hand quilt decorative motifs in special areas.

TYING

The object of tying is simply to fasten the quilt's layers together somehow every few inches. The fatter the batting, the farther apart you'll make the stitches, as a rule; but closer tying makes a quilt more durable. Use a strong needle, straight or curved (with as small a hole as you can thread), a thimble, and scissors. Stitching away from seams is easier, but stitching where seams come together is a way to hide seams that don't line up well. If you choose to stitch through seams, use a pair of pliers to help pull the needle through the layers of fabric.

Tying is a versatile technique you can adapt to many conditions or materials. Here are some things we have experimented with or heard of other people doing.

WAYS TO SPREAD OUT THE QUILT

◆ Stretch it on a quilting frame, especially if you have helpers.

◆ Spread it on the floor, so you can vacuum up the clippings.

◆ Spread it on a tabletop that won't be damaged by the needle; it's easy to tell when the needle has gone through all layers.

◆ Spread it on a bed, but you'll need a hand underneath (ouch!), and you'll have to be careful not to stitch the quilt to the bed-spread.

TIE THE QUILT WITH . . .

✦ *Crochet cotton,* if basic colors are okay.

✦ *Embroidery floss,* if you want special colors (use all six strands of thread).

✦ *Yarn. Caution:* some types ball up with washing; test a sample first. To thread the yarn (1) cut a few inches of regular thread and a yard or two of yarn; (2) fold over the thread and poke the ends through the needle's eye, leaving a loop; (3) poke the end of the yarn through the loop of thread; and (4) pull the thread back through the eye, bringing a loop of yarn through as you go.

✦ *Ribbon,* ¹/₈" *wide.* Cut the ends diagonally and treat with Fray Check; use short lengths to avoid wear and tear. Ribbon tends to come untied, so tie in a double knot, then a bow knot, and then tie the loops again.

✦ *Embellishments.* Use heavy thread and with each stitch fasten on a button or a bead. Or to each stitch, add a length of yarn or ribbon, which you then tie in a decorative way.

Basic Tying Routines

Choose the routine that fits the number of helpers you have and their skill. (We'll use the word *floss,* but remember you can use other materials.)

✦ *Group tying.* One person does threads the needle, one does the stitching, one clips the floss midway between the stitches, one ties the ends together with a square knot (or any other secure knot), and one clips ends of the floss to a uniform length (about 1").

✦ *Efficient and frugal one-person tying.* Using large stitches, stitch in and out until you run out of floss (leave the needle attached). Go back to the first stitch and clip the floss, leaving just enough length to tie the first knot. Pull up slack with the needle, clip the floss, and tie the second knot. Repeat until done. You should free up enough floss to make a few more stitches before rethreading the needle. With practice, you'll learn to cut just the right length for each knot; you won't need to trim the tufts

after tying and you won't have any clippings to clean up.

✦ *Tie-as-you-go.* Take a short stitch, tie a knot, take the next stitch, tie the knot. When you're finished, the threads need to be clipped—do this yourself or ask your FLP to cut the threads and trim the tag ends to a uniform length.

MACHINE QUILTING

Machine quilting is an art you can spend years developing, but simple quilting isn't difficult. Children's quilts that will be used every day are a great place to practice for the masterpiece you may make someday. If you don't have machine quilting experience or reference books to guide you, use the following tips.

Quilt with fairly large stitches. Start and end a line of stitching with tiny stitches or with backstitching. Roll up the extra bulk of the quilt, if necessary, so that it'll fit under the machine.

Before starting a quilt in the morning for a baby shower that night, determine if you can quilt it quickly! Straight lines and gentle curves are the fastest way to go. It's often quicker to quilt away from the seam lines than to try to keep the stitching "in the ditch" (in the seam line). For a more complicated quilt or a wallhanging, plan to stitch an interesting pattern that complements the patchwork. Often a design that fills a particular space but does not follow the seam lines is best. If you have the time and skill, stitching in the ditch can be a fine way to quilt a project.

In this Sailboat Quilt, I combined free-motion quilting (for the clouds and water) with straight quilting (to outline and detail the boats and in the borders). For more on Sailboat blocks, see Chapter 5. The Pinwheel block in the corner is from my book Fast Patch: A Treasury of Strip Quilt Projects (see the Appendix); it's a variation of the Ohio Star block.

PREPARING TO QUILT

✦ Layer your quilt as described on page 12.

✦ Baste thoroughly with thread or pin with safety pins every 5" to 8".

✦ Fill a couple of extra bobbins with your quilting thread so you won't have to remove the quilt from the machine to rewind bobbins.

Free-Motion Quilting

Use a "darning" setting (if you have one) or otherwise adjust your machine so the feed dogs are lowered. (On some machines, you cover the feed dogs; set the stitch length to 0, or the cover will pop off!)

The basic idea is to move the quilt back and forth and side to side as you sew, but not to rotate it. You should end up with smooth-looking curves. Free-motion quilting takes a lot of practice, and some machines are much better at this than others. Practice on prequilted fabric such as old place mats. The Big Foot, available for some machines, looks like a big transparent circle instead of a regular foot; this helps you see where you're going and makes it easier to avoid sewing tucks (in the front of the quilt at least).

Nancy Foisy of Coos Bay, Oregon, makes each of her grandchildren a quilt with his or her birth announcement stitched into it by machine or by hand. I'd like to get good enough at free-motion quilting so that I could stitch secret messages in the quilts I make for my grandchildren. If they still have the quilts when they are old enough to read cursive writing, the messages and the quilts may have a special meaning for them.

For really special free-motion quilting, try Hari Walner's continuous quilting designs. These are available through Beautiful Publications, 13340 Harrison Street, Thornton, CO 80241-1403 (or call 303-452-3337). Ask for the children's collection.

For now, we usually do stippling quilting. Let the path of stitching meander around to create a pattern that resembles a jigsaw puzzle. It should look something like this:

The line of stitching should not cross itself. If you find that you've stitched yourself into a dead end, start over somewhere else.

Straight Line Quilting

Many of the quilts in this book are variations of Checkerboards, on point or straight. It's easiest to quilt them with straight lines at 45° angles from the squares, as shown.

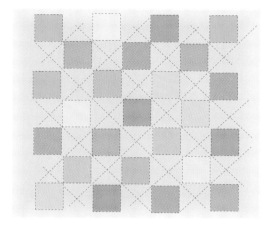

If you want to outline a design, it's easiest to sew 1/4" from the seams. Sometimes you might want to stitch in the ditch; we use this mostly for borders and with darker fabrics where mistakes won't show as much.

If you're going to do a lot of machine quilting, consider getting a walking foot (also called an "even-feed" foot), if one is available for your machine. Otherwise take care to keep the top and bottom layers of your quilt feeding in at the same rate.

Gentle Curves

A third technique is sort of compromise of the other two. Sew in gentle curves between the shapes. Set the feed dogs down or up and use an even-feed foot or not, whichever works best for you and your machine. Here's how we would machine quilt a Jiffy Quilt (page 28):

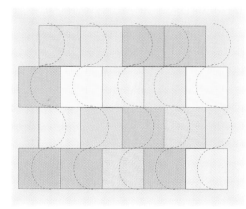

FINISHING THE QUILT

TRADITIONAL BINDING

Bind children's quilts with a durable fabric or be prepared to replace the binding when it wears. Here are some suggestions for how to put a double-layer binding on straight fabric.

1 Trim the edges. After you have finished quilting the project, spread it out flat and trim the three layers of the quilt flush with each other.

2 Prepare the binding. Find the distance around the edges of the quilt. Cut enough 2 1/2"-wide fabric strips so that when they are joined they'll create one strip that is several inches longer than the distance around the quilt. (Most of the quilts in this book will need four or five 44"-long strips.) Piece the strips together with angled seams. Fold the binding over into a double layer, right side out.

3 Fold over and pin in place. Pin the binding to the right side of the quilt if you will be hand stitching it to finish (for wallhangings and better quilts). Pin it to the wrong side of the quilt if you will be machine stitching the second side.

Starting somewhere other than a corner, match the raw edges of the binding to the edges of the quilt. Fold over the short end of the strip—to the top—so the raw edge will be covered when you fold the binding to the other side of the quilt. Pin the binding in place along one side of the quilt.

4 Stitch. The placement of the stitching line depends on how thick the quilt is, so do a test first. Start with a 3/8" seam allowance and sew along the edge of the quilt through all the layers of fabric. Stop after a few inches and check the binding. Adjust the seam allowance, if necessary; the folded edge of the binding should come right to the stitching line on the other side of the quilt. Sew the along the first side of the quilt.

5 Turn the corners carefully. Stop 3/8" from the corner of the quilt and remove the work from the machine.

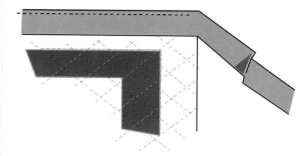

6 Fold the binding back so the fold covers the last stitches you made and is even with the edge of the quilt. Skip over the fold and try to put the needle right next to where you left off.

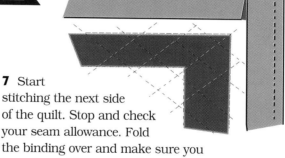

7 Start stitching the next side of the quilt. Stop and check your seam allowance. Fold the binding over and make sure you have the right amount of slack to get a neat corner. It is better if your binding is snug enough to give the quilt slightly rounded corners than to have too much slack, which gives dog-eared corners. It takes practice to know just how much binding to fold back to keep the corners neat.

8 Continue stitching around the quilt, repeating these steps at each corner. When you reach the beginning point, overlap the binding slightly, to hide the raw edges of the end of the binding.

9 Stitch the other side. Fold binding over the edge of the quilt and pin it in place on the other side. Stitch the second side down by hand or machine.

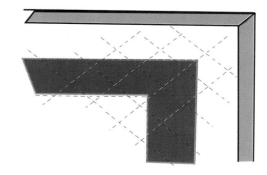

Involving Kids

Here's how to get your FLP involved, even if she is very young or doesn't have the attention span to see a quilt through from start to finish. To let the child see some immediate results, cut out and sew together the pieces for just one block, instead of using the strip-piecing method to create many blocks. Or try sewing up just a small section of the quilt. If your FLP leaves and making the quilt is no longer a social occasion, you'll be able to finish it quickly with the strip-piecing method. This way, the youngster can still feel proud of her contribution to the whole quilt.

USING THE QUICK-TURN METHOD FOR FINISHING EDGES

Betsy and others who make quilts to sell often turn a quilt instead of adding a binding, especially for quilts that will have a puffy batting and will be tied. The quilt shown on page 12 was finished with this method. If the final border is about 1" wide and is the same fabric as the back of the quilt, you can create the impression of an applied binding.

1 Spread out the quilt layers on a large cutting mat. First spread out the batting. Then lay the backing over it right side up. Finally spread out the quilt top, making sure it is right side down.

2 Using the rotary cutter, trim all the layers to the same size. Use the lines on your ruler to keep the borders even on all sides. Move your cutting mat along as you go, if necessary.

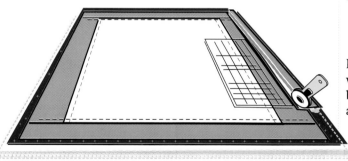

3 Machine stitch around the quilt. Pin the layers together in several places and stitch ½" in from the edges. If your stitching tends to draw up the fabric slightly, that's okay; that will help keep edges from ruffling later. Leave a 14" to 18" opening in the middle of one end of the quilt. Then staystitch the fabric at the opening, stitching the batting and backing together.

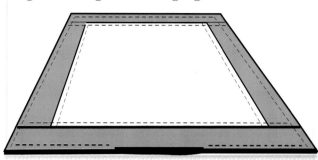

4 Turn the quilt right side out through the opening. Straighten the edges; it may help to reach inside the opening. Pin the opening closed, folding the raw edges to the inside.

5 Stitch the opening shut by hand.

6 Top stitch around the edge of the quilt, ½" to 1" in from the edge. (Stitch along the seam of the final border, if you are creating the illusion of an applied binding.)

7 Tie the project or quilt it lightly. Don't do heavy quilting on a quick-turned quilt, since that would bunch up the center of the quilt and make the edges ruffle.

THE FINAL TOUCH—SIGN YOUR QUILT

When your quilt is finished, sign your name. If you like, add the date; special details, such as who the quilt was made for; and its title, if you believe in naming quilts. Sign the front or back, as large or small as you please; use quilting stitches, embroidery thread, or indelible ink. ★

CHAPTER THREE

Playing with Blocks

Making blocks is fun, finishing the quilt is rewarding, but in between is the best step of all—arranging your blocks. There are so many possibilities that this step gets its own chapter.

If you have time, you can spread out your patchwork blocks over every pretty piece of fabric you have, trying one arrangement after another. Is this a good color for sashing? Or would it be better to have big plain blocks from this other fabric? Play with the blocks for hours, if you wish, with your Favorite Little People helping and giving their opinions.

You may have started a project with a certain layout in mind, but be sure to try some others. You could discover a dynamite look you hadn't expected. Changing your mind is what makes quiltmaking fun, not work. You don't need to put your blocks together the way some person or book says to (even if *you* are the person who decided, a few hours or days ago, you would do things a certain way).

All these quilts were made by Betsy. Grandma's Secret (top left) is from Chapter 4 and the Dinosaur Quilt (top right) repeats one of the blocks presented in Chapter 7. The Nine Patch Quilt (bottom left), which is set with the blocks adjacent to each other, and the Storybook Quilt (bottom right) are described in this chapter.

SOME SIMPLE BLOCK ARRANGEMENTS

In the last chapter, we showed you how to strip-piece simple Nine Patch and Checkerboard blocks. We'll use those blocks now to demonstrate some basic block arrangements.

SETTING BLOCKS WITH SASHING

Sashing refers to the borders between blocks. Assemble rows of blocks with *short* sashing between the blocks; then assemble the rows into a quilt top with *long* sashing between the rows.

If sashing reminds you of city streets, think about the "intersections." You could put contrasting squares there to add more color.

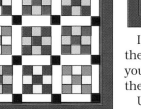

Is the first border part of the sashing, too? Maybe you'll want extra squares there, like this (at left).

Use the table on the following page to help you plan out the sashing for your quilt project.

Kelly Heath is spreading out Nine Patch blocks to choose a nice fabric for the plain blocks.

Large-scale blocks like this are easy for children to help with. If you're making a scrap version, get your Favorite Little Person to help you choose the fabrics.

18 Pieced Blocks Used with 17 Plain Blocks

This arrangement of Nine Patch blocks is called Irish Chain because of the way the dark squares chain diagonally across the quilt.

ALTERNATING WITH PLAIN BLOCKS

A quick way to make a project larger is to alternate the patchwork blocks with plain blocks. How you decide to *quilt* the project becomes more important when you have big empty squares to embellish, so plan ahead.

The effect of quilt top is nicer when there is a patchwork block in each corner, which means that you have an odd number of blocks in both directions. Here are two good combinations.

8 Pieced Blocks Used with 7 Plain Blocks

Use a large block since so few units are needed to complete the quilt top. Our example is shown with strip-pieced Checkerboard blocks.

You can use only two colors for the entire quilt top, or you can use a variety of colors (as shown) but only two colors in each block. Make sets of three blocks in six different color combinations, as on page 10.

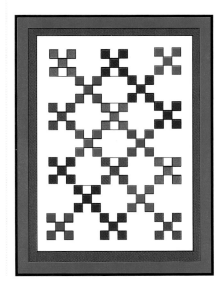

SETTING BLOCKS NEXT TO EACH OTHER

If you set pieced blocks right next to other pieced blocks you'll need to sew more carefully so the seams line up. Stick with one of the other arrangements if time is short or a child is helping. But many wonderful scrap quilts are set without sashing.

When using Nine Patch blocks, the blocks that touch should have the dark and light squares in the opposite positions. Make the blocks with distinct color differences, and have some of the "light" fabrics actually be *medium* to help make individual blocks stand out.

Fussing with the blocks is fun if you have your Favorite Little Person to do the stooping and crawling to switch blocks. (Remember, any arrangement your FLP likes is automatically perfect.) If you're in a hurry and don't want to fuss, just use the same blocks in the first, third, and fifth rows. Use a second set of blocks in the second, fourth, and sixth rows. Mix up the positions within the rows. (But please don't be a slave to this "rule"; mix up the blocks a little more if you wish.)

SETTING BLOCKS ON POINT

To set a block "on point" means to turn the blocks so the edges run at a 45° angle to the edges of the quilt. You can get a wonderful dynamic look this way, and a few blocks go a long way if pieced blocks alternate with plain blocks. This is the best arrangement for most of the Nine Patch Nature blocks in Chapter 6.

Lay out your rows diagonally, as shown, so you can easily sew the rows together with long seams.

The grain line is straight along the edges of the quilt. The triangles at the sides of the blocks are cut extra large to allow plenty of overlap. Just trim off any surplus when you square up the quilt top.

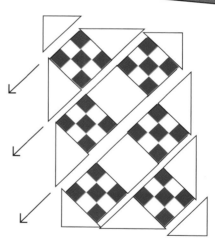

SASHING

Number of Blocks Used	Number of Sashing Strips— no Contrasting Squares		Number of Sashing Strips— with Contrasting Squares		Number of Sashing Strips— Contrasting Squares in Border	
	SHORT	LONG	SASHING	SQUARES	SASHING	SQUARES
9 (3×3)	6	2	12	4	24	16
12 (3×4)	8	3	17	6	31	20
15 (3×5)	10	4	22	8	38	24
16 (4×4)	12	3	24	9	40	25
20 (4×5)	15	4	31	12	49	30
24 (4×6)	18	5	38	15	58	35
25 (5×5)	20	4	40	16	60	36
30 (5×6)	25	5	49	20	71	42
36 (6×6)	30	5	60	25	84	49
42 (6×7)	35	6	71	30	97	56

PLANNING QUILTS WITH BLOCKS SET ON POINT

These quilts use four different types of elements: pieced blocks, plain blocks, side triangles, and corner triangles. The table below lists how many you need of each.

ELEMENTS FOR QUILTS SET ON POINT

Number of Pieced Blocks	Number of Plain Blocks	Number of Side Triangles	Number of Corner Triangles
6 (2 × 3)	2	6	4
12 (3 × 4)	6	10	4
15 (3 × 5)	8	12	4
16 (4 × 4)	9	12	4
24 (4 × 6)	15	16	4
35 (5 × 7)	24	20	4
40 (5 × 8)	28	22	4

MAKING SIDE AND CORNER TRIANGLES

To make the side triangles, cut large squares in fourths. To make the corner triangles, cut smaller squares in half.

The following table shows what size to cut the squares so they'll match the pieced blocks and also include the seam allowances. The measurements are generous in case of error.

SIZES FOR QUILTS SET ON POINT

Block Size (INCLUDING SEAM ALLOWANCES)	Squares for the Side Triangles (CUT IN FOURTHS, DIAGONALLY)	Squares for the Corner Triangles (CUT IN HALF, DIAGONALLY)
4"	7"	4"
5"	8"	5"
6"	10"	6"
7"	11"	6"
8"	12"	7"
9"	14"	8"
10"	16"	8"
11"	17"	9"

Here are two shortcuts to simplify the stacking and cutting of layers of fabric:

◆ **Shortcut 1.** If you have two leftover side triangles, cut each in half once more to make the four corners. (They'll be just barely large enough.)

◆ **Shortcut 2.** Make two extra plain blocks and cut each diagonally one time for the four corners. They'll be a little larger than you need, but this method simplifies the cutting, so just trim off the extra fabric.

SETTING ADJACENT BLOCKS ON POINT

If you are making Nine Patch blocks, don't use the same number of dark-corner blocks as light-corner blocks; instead use the table "Elements for Quilts Set on Point" at left. To determine the number of dark-cornered squares you need, look in the column labeled "Number of Pieced Blocks"; for light-cornered blocks, look in the column labeled "Number of Plain Blocks." Make the side and corner triangles out of solid fabric.

USE THE DANCING SQUARES SHORTCUT TO SET A QUILT ON POINT

The Dancing Squares shortcut (described on page 32) can also be used to set the blocks on point. You sew up a quilt top with an even number of blocks going the long direction, and then set it on point instantly by making two diagonal cuts. The outer blocks will lose their corners in the seams, but most children won't notice.

A SURPRISE VARIATION— THE STORYBOOK QUILT

For this quilt, patchwork blocks alternate with colorful pictures. If you are artistic and have time, decorate the squares with paints or stencils, or use pictures made with fabric crayons by your FLP. But if you want a quick quilt, use a printed fabric and make one of our Storybook Quilts. We've added a special twist— small squares placed along two sides of each picture.

CHOOSING THE PICTURES

Choose the pictures first, then make the rest of the quilt to fit. Take your Favorite Little Person along with you to the fabric store (allow an hour or so at the store) and have fun. Before leaving home, make a viewfinder from a couple of file folders. Cut two L-shaped pieces with inside measurements of 9" or more. To use the viewfinder, overlap the two L's over different printed fabrics, adjusting their positions to see what size blocks would look best.

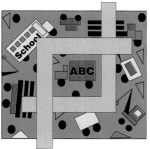

Be sure to let your FLP point out his

favorite fabrics. Don't worry too much about the grain of the fabric. Just turn your viewfinder any which way to isolate some nice pictures.

Starting with Square Pictures

Here are some sizes of square Storybook pictures that work well. The 5", 7 1/2", and 10 1/2" squares are featured in the three projects we present in this chapter.

✦ If you find **5"-*square pictures,*** use 10 of them to make the Nine Patch Storybook Quilt presented in this chapter. Start with 5 1/2" squares (before seams).

✦ If you find **6"-*square pictures,*** use 10 of them to make the Nine Patch Storybook Quilt. Start with 6 1/2" squares (before seams). Alter the directions in the chapter by using 3 1/2"-wide strips.

✦ If you find **6 3/4"-*square pictures,*** use 6 of them to make the Checkerboard Storybook Quilt. Start with 7 1/4" squares (before seams). Alter the directions in the chapter by using 2 3/4"-wide strips.

✦ If you find **7 1/2"-*square pictures,*** use 6 of them to make the Checkerboard Storybook Quilt presented in this chapter. Start with 8" squares (before seams).

✦ If you find **9"-*square pictures,*** use 12 of them for the Twin Storybook Quilt. Start with 9 1/2" squares (before seams). Alter the directions in the chapter by using 3 1/2"-wide strips.

✦ If you find **10 1/2"-*square pictures,*** use 12 of them to make the Twin Storybook Quilt in this chapter. Start with 11" squares (before seams).

Starting with Rectangular Pictures

If you find Storybook rectangles rather than squares, add small squares to one side of the Storybook block only. Either don't use the shorter chains at all or use the chains of extra squares to make the quilt larger. The following sizes will be easiest to adapt.

✦ If you find **5" × 7 1/2"** *rectangles,* make a Nine Patch Storybook Quilt using 10 pictures.

✦ If you find **7 1/2" × 10"** *rectangles,* make a Checkerboard Storybook Quilt using 6 pictures.

✦ If you find **7" × 10 1/2"** *rectangles,* make a Twin Storybook Quilt using 12 pictures. For this quilt, make more chains and use them on three sides of the pictures, not just two.

This Checkerboard Storybook Quilt was made by Anita. Did you spot the error in the top right corner? Don't deliberately make mistakes, but don't worry if you do; they can make a quilt more interesting.

CHOOSING THE OTHER FABRICS

The fabrics for the strip-pieced blocks should be color coordinated with the Storybook blocks. But avoid using the same color that was used for the *background* of the pictures.

For each project, strip-pieced fabrics will be on two "teams": A and B. If you're new to strip-piecing, be sure you have read Chapter 2.

GENERAL INSTRUCTIONS FOR THE STORYBOOK QUILTS

These basic directions apply to all three Storybook projects.

Strip-Piecing the Blocks

Review the directions for making Nine Patch and Checkerboard blocks in Chapter 2. Instead of light and dark, use A and B strips (an equal number of each). Sew as directed in each project, and then cut cross-sections. Assemble the blocks, mixing up the sections randomly. Follow the illustrations carefully, keeping the A and B colors in the right positions.

After making all the Nine Patch or Checkerboard blocks you need, add squares to two sides of each picture. Add short chains to the *left* side of the picture in half the blocks and to the *right* side in the other blocks. Then add chains to the *top* of half the blocks and to the *bottom* of the others.

Use the leftover pieces to make a long chain of squares to sew to the bottom of the quilt.

Arranging the Blocks

Lay out patchwork blocks and picture blocks to find a nice arrangement. Ask your FLP to help place the picture blocks.

Try to keep the A and B colors in consistent positions in each block so you get a nice diagonal progression of A colors across the quilt in one direction and B colors in the other direction.

✦ Don't let the picture blocks touch the edge of the quilt top. Also try to have animals and people face the center of the quilt.

Finishing the Quilt

Sew everything together, with your FLP handing you the sections, then returning them to the arrangement after you sew them.

Add borders and complete the quilt, using the suggestions given in Chapter 2.

MACHINE QUILTING TIP

Stitch around the picture blocks and borders, then stitch diagonally in both directions through the small squares, but not through the pictures. Add more quilting inside each picture block, if you wish.

NINE PATCH STORYBOOK QUILT

For this project you'll need 10 Nine Patch blocks, 10 Storybook blocks, and a chain of squares made from the leftover units. This quilt will be about 30"×40" before you add borders and about 40"×50" with the borders.

FABRIC NEEDED

✦ Enough of the graphic print fabric to cut out 10 pictures, each 5 1/2" square (white in our example).

✦ For Team A: scraps or fat quarters of about eight fabrics in one color family (blues and greens in our example).

✦ For Team B: 5/8 yard or scraps of a color that contrasts with Team A (red and pink in example).

✦ About 1/3 yard of each border fabric.

✦ Binding fabric, backing fabric, and batting; the amount needed depends on the width of your borders (see Chapter 2).

MAKING THE QUILT TOP

1 Cut 11 strips of A fabrics and 11 of B fabrics, each 3"×22".

2 Sew the strips together to make eight panels as shown, and then press the seams toward the A (or darker) fabrics.

Two sets of two strips: A-B

Three sets of three strips: A-B-A

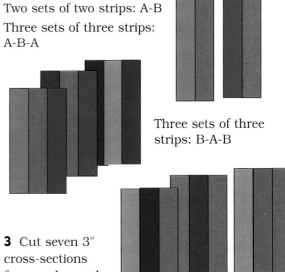

Three sets of three strips: B-A-B

3 Cut seven 3" cross-sections from each panel.

4 Make 10 Nine Patch blocks with color A in the corners (see page 10).

5 Make 10 Storybook blocks.

   a Measure the two-square chains, and cut the picture blocks to that size (about 5 1/2" square).

   b Sew a two-square chain to each picture,

with color A in the upper position in some blocks and in the lower position for other blocks, referring to the figure below.

c Add a three-square chain above or below each picture unit, again watching the placement of A and B colors. Use the figure below.

6 Arrange the blocks.

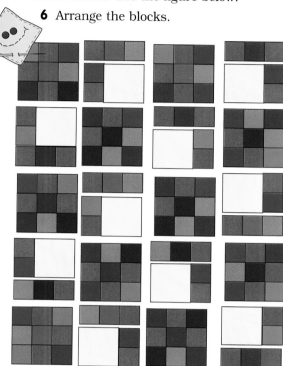

7 Sew the blocks together and finish the quilt as suggested on page 22.

CHECKERBOARD STORYBOOK QUILT

This quilt has six 8" pictures, six 4"×4" Checkerboards, and a chain of squares. The Checkerboard Storybook Quilt will be about 30"×43" before you add borders and about 40"×53" with the borders.

FABRIC NEEDED

✦ Enough of the graphic print to cut out six pictures, each 8" square (light blue in our example).

✦ For Team A: scraps or fat quarters in eight different fabrics of one color family (blues and greens in our example).

✦ For Team B: 5/8 yard of one color or scraps of a different color family (pinks and reds in our example).

✦ About 1/3 yard of each border fabric.

✦ Binding fabric, backing fabric, and batting;

the amount needed depends on the width of your borders (see Chapter 2).

MAKING THE QUILT TOP

1 Cut 11 strips of A fabrics and 11 strips of B fabrics, each 3"×22".

2 Sew strips together to make six panels. First sew five sets of four strips (A-B-A-B).

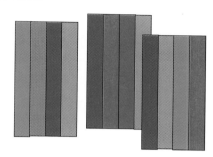

3 Cut three individual 3" squares off the end of each of the two strips left over and set them aside. Now sew what's left of these two strips to each other.

4 Cut each panel into 3" cross-sections. This makes 35 chains of four squares and four sets of two squares.

5 Make six 4×4 Checker-board blocks (see page 10).

6 Cut out six picture blocks. To determine the exact size of the pictures, shorten two of the leftover chains of four by removing one square. Measure the three-square chain, and cut the picture blocks to that size (about 8" square).

7 Finish the Storybook blocks.

a Add three-square chains. You'll need six chains of three; use the two chains you made in Step 6 and make four more chains of three by sewing the reserved squares (Step 3) to the chains of two.

b Add four-square chains. Lay out a four-square chain next to each picture block unit, referring to the picture on the next page. Place the squares in Team A in the top left-hand corner each time. If the picture itself is in the top left-hand corner, the Team A square should be in the bottom right-hand corner.

NOTE.

In one sample Storybook Quilt I made—before I had discovered this rule—I had some squares in the wrong position, and it threw the color sequence off. The mistake wasn't obvious, so I didn't correct it. Look at the photo on page 21, and see if you can spot the error.

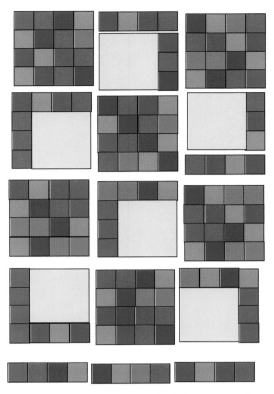

8 Arrange the blocks, sew the blocks together, and finish the quilt as suggested on page 22.

TWIN STORYBOOK QUILT

For this quilt you'll need 12 Storybook pictures (each 11" square) and 12 Checkerboard blocks (made from 4"-wide strips). This quilt will be about 56" × 88" without the borders. Note that the Twin Storybook Quilt is simply a larger version of the Checkerboard Storybook Quilt. Read through the directions for the smaller quilt first (page 23) and then follow the adapted steps below.

FABRIC NEEDED

✦ Enough of the graphic print to cut out 12 pictures, each 11" square (red in our example).

IQ Builder

Sometime, maybe months after you've finished your Storybook Quilt, give your FLP a puzzle that will help her recognize sequences.

Cut a sheet of colored paper into seven strips about 1" wide. Looking at your quilt, pick out four squares you recognize as being part of a chain and lay the paper strip over those four colors. Ask the child if she can find more chains with colors in the same sequence and place a paper strip over them. If she likes the challenge, cut strips of other colors and have her look for other chains.

✦ For Team A: ¼ yard or scraps of 8 to 15 fabrics in a dark color (greens and blues in our example).

✦ For Team B: 1 ²/₃ yards or scraps of 8 to 15 fabrics in a light color (white in our example).

✦ About ½ yard of each border fabric.

✦ Binding fabric, backing fabric, and batting; the amount needed depends on the width of your borders (see Chapter 2).

MAKING THE QUILT TOP

1 Cut 15 strips of A fabrics and 15 strips of B fabrics, each 4" × 44".

2 Sew the strips together to make eight panels. Six sets of four strips: A-B-A-B

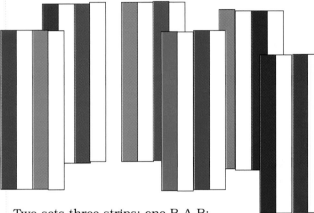

Two sets three strips: one B-A-B; one A-B-A

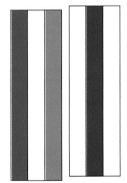

3 Cut ten 4" cross-sections from each panel.

4 Make 12 Checkerboard blocks. Use 48 of the four-square chains to make the 4 × 4 blocks.

5 Make 12 Storybook blocks.

a Measure one of three-square chains and cut 12 picture blocks to that size (about 11" square).

b Sew a chain of three squares to the left or right side of each picture block, using six chains of each color sequence and referring to the picture on the next page.

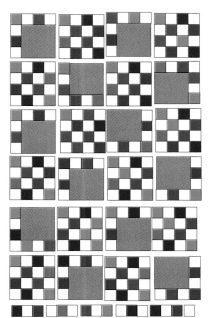

c Sew a four-square chain to the top or bottom of each picture unit, making sure a Team A square is in the top left-hand corner or bottom right-hand corner each time, as shown.

4 Arrange the blocks. Your FLP will probably have definite ideas about how to arrange the Storybook blocks—just ask him!

5 Sew the blocks together and finish the quilt as suggested on page 22.

CREATIVE ARRANGEMENTS

Once you get the hang of sewing the blocks together to make a quilt top, you can use your imagination to come up with many other unique arrangements. Here are some ideas and tips to get you started.

✦ ***Mix blocks from different chapters.*** Try alternating simple Nine Patch blocks (with low color contrast) with the Nine Patch Nature blocks shown in Chapter 6.

✦ ***Make a "What's-on-Hand" Quilt.*** If you have leftover blocks from several quilt project, one-of-a-kind picture blocks, and

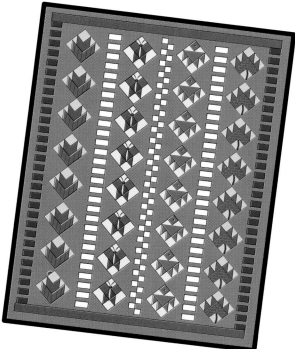

scraps of plain fabric, you can just make up your own arrangement. This quilt was made from recycled blue jeans and stenciled dinosaurs. Kids really have fun arranging the blocks for a What's-on-Hand Quilt.

✦ ***Make a "Strippy" Quilt.*** This strippy quilt uses blocks from Chapter 6. Although this quilt has vertical rows, horizontal rows look just as nice.

✦ ***Make a Medallion Quilt.*** These stunning quilts start with a central block or cluster of blocks. You build up the quilt by adding borders made up of other blocks. See the photo of Pam Dittmar's quilt on page 63 and the diagrams on page 62 for examples. ★

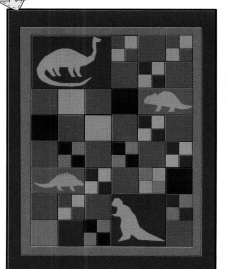

David Heath, at age six, helps Betsy choose blocks for a What's-on-Hand Quilt.

CHAPTER FOUR

Dancing Squares

Many of the everyday quilts throughout the years have been made up of simple squares. Great-Grandma would have pieced them from small pieces of whatever wool or cotton she had on hand, but you don't have to. You can get the same look much faster with strip-piecing.

David Heath (at age four) on the playground with his Dancing Squares Quilt and his brother Joseph (age 2 at the time). We don't recommend taking your quilts outside (except to photograph them), because the sun and dirt aren't good for them.

CHECKERBOARD QUILTS

Some of the simplest quilts are basically Checkerboards, squares of dark and light alternating with each other. (Actually, we usually alternate between *light* and *medium* or between *medium* and *dark* or between *warm* and *cool* colors.) The following table includes typical sizes; you probably won't make squares any larger or smaller than the ones listed, but you can certainly use a different number of squares. Remember, borders make quilts much larger.

TWO-COLOR CHECKERBOARD QUILT

This is an 8×12 Checkerboard made from 4" squares. It's about 28"×42" before the borders. When strip-piecing a small quilt like this, use only two colors.

FABRIC NEEDED

+ 1 yard of a dark fabric (includes enough for one border).

+ 1 yard of a light fabric (includes enough for one border).

+ Binding fabric, backing fabric, and batting; the amount depends on the width of your borders (see Chapter 2).

NOTE:
We usually use full 44" strips when making our quilts, but sometimes the math works out better with shorter strips. For this quilt, the strips are 33". Before cutting the strips, remove an 11"×44" piece from each fabric and set it aside for the borders. Then remove another 11" from each fabric, leaving 25"×33" pieces for cutting your strips.

MAKING THE QUILT TOP

1 Cut six strips of dark fabric and six strips of light fabric, each 4"×33".

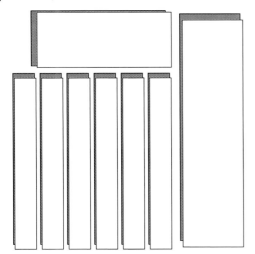

2 Sew all the strips together into one big panel, alternating light and dark strips.

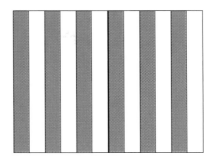

3 Cut cross-sections from the panel. Fold over the panel so it'll fit on your cutting mat and under your ruler. Square up one end and cut eight 4" cross-sections.

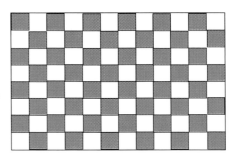

4 Reverse half the chains, and sew them together again.

5 Add borders—*maybe*. Be sure to read the rest of this chapter because you might change your mind. If you decide to keep the Checker-

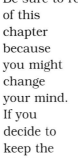

board as it is, add borders and finish the quilt as desired. For tips on assembling and finishing your quilt, see Chapter 2.

MACHINE QUILTING TIP
Quilt diagonally through the dark squares using a dark thread and through the light squares using a light thread.

SIZES OF CHECKERBOARD QUILTS (WITHOUT BORDERS)

Width of Strips	Square Size (after seams)	96 Squares (8×12)	140 Squares (10×14)	192 Squares (12×16)	336 Squares (14×20)
3"	2 1/2"	20×30"	25×35"	30×40"	35×50"
3 1/2"	3"	24×36"	30×42"	36×48"	42×60"
4"	3 1/2"	28×42"	35×49"	42×56"	49×70"
4 1/2"	4"	32×48"	40×56"	48×64"	56×80"
5"	4 1/2"	36×54"	45×63"	54×72"	63×90"

FLANNEL SCRAP QUILT

Here's a soft, cuddly quilt that Betsy made in just a few hours. (A durable version of this quilt—good for donating to shelters for the homeless—could be made of recycled blue jeans or other tough fabric.) It's hard to get a random scrap look in a small project like this. Betsy's quilt works because the colors are low contrast and the same colors are repeated in different fabrics. We'll call the strips light and dark, even though Betsy's "darks" are actually pastel. This quilt measures 36"×50" with one narrow border.

This Flannel Scrap Quilt was pieced by Betsy. She lined her quilt with flannel and machine quilted it along the seams of the squares.

FABRIC NEEDED

✦ Scraps of 7 to 14 different dark or medium flannel prints.

✦ 1 yard light flannel (or use more scraps).

✦ 1/4 to 1/3 yard of each border fabric.

✦ Binding fabric, backing fabric, and batting; the amount needed depends on the width of your borders (see Chapter 2).

MAKING THE QUILT TOP

1 Cut 14 strips of light fabrics and 14 strips of dark fabrics, each 4"×21" (or 22").

2 Sew the strips together to make four panels of seven strips each. Make two panels with dark strips on the edges, and two with light strips.

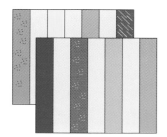
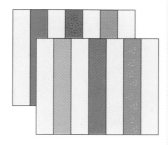

3 Square up one end of each panel. Cut each panel into 4" cross-sections.

4 Find a nice arrangement. Mix up the chains and then lay them out, matching two chains end to end at a time.

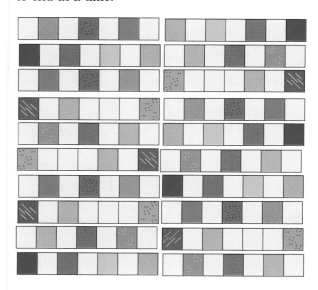

5 Join the chains in pairs to make 10 chains with 14 squares in each.

6 Sew all chains together to make the quilt top.

7 Add borders and finish the quilt as desired. For tips, see Chapter 2.

QUILTING TIPS

Quilt in the ditch, outlining each square; tie the quilt with a tuft of yarn in the middle of each square; or machine quilt by sewing diagonally through all the squares.

JIFFY QUILT

This is another cozy, unpretentious quilt. No sitting around waiting to become an heirloom for this quilt: Your Favorite Little Person can use it every day. Instead of alternating between light and dark, use random colors, bright prints, and solids.

Most quilts need careful cutting and sewing so the seams will line up. The "orderly" version of the Jiffy Quilt does too. But if this is your first quilt or your FLP is going to help, do the "offset" version, where seams don't have to line up. This is the best project in the book for a child learning to use the sewing machine. You'll still need to help with the cutting.

If you are experienced, you can make quick gifts for a lot of children with the Jiffy Quilt. Piece each quilt top in a couple of hours, use the quick-turn method to finish the edges (Chapter 2), and tie the quilts.

If no borders are added, you'll have a crib quilt that measures about 33"×52". Add several borders to make a twin bed throw of about 53"×72". (Remember, it'll be smaller after quilting.)

FABRIC NEEDED

✦ ⅛ yard of 15 different fabrics (though you can use fewer colors).

✦ ½ to ⅔ yard for each border fabric.

✦ Binding fabric, backing fabric, and batting; the amount needed depends on the width of your borders and whether you are using the quick-turn method (see Chapter 2).

MAKING THE QUILT TOP

1 Cut 15 strips (all different fabrics, if possible), each 4"× 44".

2 Sew the strips together to make three panels of five strips each. You can do this quickly, but to make arranging the squares easier, follow these rules:

a Watch the edge colors. Don't use a similar fabric on the edges of two sets.

b Don't use fabrics that will totally clash with each other on the edges.

c If you use the same fabric twice—or two very similar fabrics—put one of them in the center of one panel, and the other on the edge of a different panel.

Sara (age ten) and Julie (age eight) Knifton made this Jiffy Quilt for their friends Jessie and Jeanine Ortiz, all from Springfield, Oregon. Neither girl had used a sewing machine before. (Left to right: Sara, Jessie, Julie, Jeanine.)

3 Cut the panels into cross-sections. Cut 4" cross-sections, making 30 chains of five squares each.

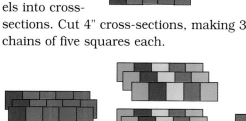

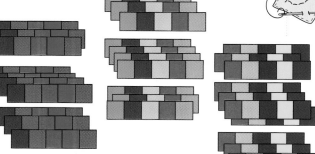

4 Sew the chains together in pairs, end to end, to make 15 chains of 10 squares each. Before sewing, turn some of the chains around and mix up the combinations in as many ways as you can.

5 Play with the chains, making sure your FLP gets a chance to help. There are two ways to sew the quilt together.

a *The Orderly Version.* Line up the seams, if your cutting and sewing are accurate and if you have time to fuss with the chains, so colors in one row don't touch the same colors in adjoining rows. You'll probably need to correct a seam occasionally for better alignment. You can undo seams and rearrange the squares for better color patterns, too.

b *The Offset Version.* Move alternate rows over 1¾" to the side. This type of quilt top is much faster to make because the seams don't need to line up, and the same colors can be used next to each other from row to row. That's what makes this such a

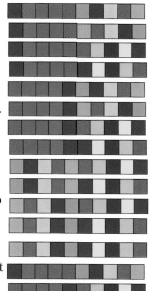

great a beginner project. Do try to distribute the colors fairly evenly.

6 Sew the chains together. If you are doing the offset version, try to line up the seams of one row with the seams two rows away. When finished, cut off the half-squares along the edges.

7 Add borders and finish the quilt as desired. For tips, see Chapter 2.

MACHINE QUILTING TIPS

Machine quilt with dark transparent thread in the needle and regular thread to match the backing in the bobbin.

For the <u>Orderly Version</u>: machine stitch diagonally through all squares. For the <u>Offset Version</u>: machine stitch from end to end in gentle curves in the middle of the squares. Start at the same end each time, and make 10 trips across the quilt.

GRANDMA'S SECRET

This colorful quilt has little Checkerboards on point. We offer two methods for making this quilt. It can be made with individual squares and triangles, if you enjoy that (or if you want to spend a lot of time with your Favorite Little Person). Otherwise, use our interesting speed-piecing method.

If you use 15 blocks, the quilt will be about 35" × 52" with one narrow inner border and a 4" outer border. We suggest that you use bright fabrics, solids, or low-contrast prints and that you not have too much contrast between the darks and lights. All the colors of the rainbow can be used in this quilt; try yellow for the sashing and use the other colors in the blocks.

FABRIC NEEDED

◆ **For the blocks:** scraps of 8 or more fabrics, enough to cut a *total* of sixteen 10" squares.

◆ **For the sashing and first border:** 1/2 to 5/8 yard of a color that contrasts with all other colors.

◆ **For the outer border:** 1/2 yard.

◆ **Binding fabric, backing fabric, and batting:** the amount depends on the width of your borders (see Chapter 2).

USING INDIVIDUAL SQUARES AND TRIANGLES

1 Cut the squares. Cut sixty 3" squares from your fabrics. Cut several in each color or, if you want the look of a charm quilt, make each square different.

2 Cut the triangles. Cut thirty 5" squares from your fabric. Cut each square in half diagonally twice, making a total of 120 triangles.

COLOR TIPS

The triangles can be a little lighter or darker than the squares for a special effect. They should have a high contrast with the sashing color, since they will be around the edges of the blocks.

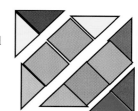

3 Assemble the squares and triangles into sets. Sew sets of two triangles together, as shown. Then sew two squares together with a triangle on each end, as shown, noting the direction of the end triangles. Your Favorite Little Person can help arrange the colors so each set has a nice mixture.

4 Join the sets into complete blocks. With the help of your FLP, arrange the parts so none of the colors will be next to the same color. Sew the blocks together, with your FLP handing you pieces, clipping them apart after they are sewn, and returning them to the arrangement.

5 Go to Step 6 under "Using the Speed-Piecing Method" on page 31 for finishing your quilt top.

USING THE SPEED-PIECING METHOD

It's easier to say "cut little pieces," but this way is quicker to do—and more interesting. For each large square you cut, you get one patchwork block. However, these directions work better with an even number of blocks, so start with 16 squares for a 15-block quilt. (You can change your mind and use all 16 blocks to make a square quilt instead. A 4×4 quilt will measure about 42" square.)

1 Cut the squares. Cut sixteen 9 1/2" squares of fabric. If you have a transparent 9 1/2" grid, just use it like a giant template. Stack four to six fabrics in pairs with right sides together. Cut a whole stack of squares at a time, and leave them carefully aligned for the next step. If you are using fewer than 16 different fabrics, pair the repeats with new colors for Step 2.

2 Cut diagonally. Cut each stack of squares diagonally down the middle. Then make a parallel cut 3" away from the first cut on both sides.

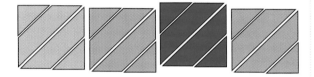

3 Sew the pieces back together into squares. Do not backstitch at ends of seams.

a First sew the longer pieces to each other. (They are already aligned in pairs and ready to go, but rearrange some of them so they have new partners.) The edges are on the bias, so pin and sew carefully to avoid stretching.

b Add the first triangle corner to all blocks. Have your FLP find a color he thinks should be added each time and hand it to you.

c Press the partial blocks. Lay them out. For each one, find a good color of triangle to complete the block—a color that hasn't been used yet in that set.

d When you are happy with all the color combinations, sew the final triangles in place.

4 Cut the other direction. Cut each pieced square down the center diagonally and then 3" from each side, as before. Pull off the bits of fabric (see the arrow in the diagram).

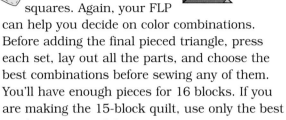

**5** Mix up the pieces and sew them back together to make new squares. Again, your FLP can help you decide on color combinations. Before adding the final pieced triangle, press each set, lay out all the parts, and choose the best combinations before sewing any of them. You'll have enough pieces for 16 blocks. If you are making the 15-block quilt, use only the best combinations and don't sew up the last block.

6 No matter which method you have used to create the blocks, trim and square them up so there is a 1/4" seam allowance on all sides.

7 Referring to "Setting Blocks with Sashing" on page 18, add the sashing and first border. Sew the quilt top together. Here's an example of a 16-block quilt.

8 Add any outer borders and finish the quilt as desired. For tips, see Chapter 2.

VARIATIONS OF GRANDMA'S SECRET

If you would like to plan other Grandma's Secret Quilts, the table below will help you with the cutting.

Here's how to make 11" Grandma's Secret blocks. You'll want to make these larger blocks if you're going to use durable fabrics, such as denim, poplin, or double-knit polyester. The

PIECES NEEDED FOR GRANDMA'S SECRET QUILTS

Number of Blocks	Arrangement	SPEED-PIECING Number of Large Squares	TRADITIONAL PIECING Number of Small Squares	Number of Triangles
12	3 × 4	12	48	96
15	3 × 5	16	60	120
16	4 × 4	16	64	128
20	4 × 5	20	80	160
24	4 × 6	24	96	192
30	5 × 6	30	120	240

sashing for these blocks can also be quite wide, so a large quilt can be made quickly.

♦ *Using Individual Squares and Triangles.* Cut 4¹/₂" squares. To make the triangles, start with 8" squares, and then cut them in fourths diagonally.

♦ *Using the Strip-Piecing Method.* Start with 13¹/₂" squares. The parallel diagonal cuts should be 4¹/₂" from the center cut (Step 2).

DANCING SQUARES

When squares are set on point, as in Grandma's Secret, they seem more alive, like they are dancing. Why do you think Harlequins had diamonds instead of squares on their tights? Make a large Checkerboard Quilt by regular strip-piecing, then give it a diagonal setting instantly with our special steps.

DANCING SQUARES QUILT

Our example uses the 8 × 12 Two-Color Checkerboard Quilt from earlier in this chapter. You could also start with Betsy's Flannel Scrap Quilt or any quilt listed in "Sizes of Checkerboard Quilts (without Borders)," on page 27. Don't use the Jiffy Quilt; unpleasant things would happen to the color scheme where edges were joined.

MAKING THE QUILT TOP

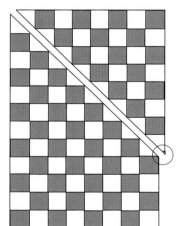

1 Cut the quilt top diagonally from any corner. The color you cut through will be along the edge of the quilt, so plan ahead. (Worried about the bias edges stretching? Draw a line where you're going cut and stay stitch ¹/₈" to ¹/₄" from the mark on both sides of the line before cutting. We don't bother.) At the edge, a straight cut lops off a little of the next square (shown in the circle). That's not a mistake; it's necessary for the seam allowances.

2 Sew the pieces together again, as shown.

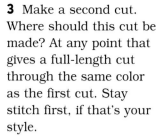

3 Make a second cut. Where should this cut be made? At any point that gives a full-length cut through the same color as the first cut. Stay stitch first, if that's your style.

CUTTING TIP

If there is a place where seams didn't line up too well, cut through that point to wipe out the mistake.

4 Sew the top together again, as shown. You've made a rectangle again, but now the squares are on point.

5 Add the borders. Note that you will lose the points of the squares when you sew borders on, but your FLP won't mind. If it bothers you, trim off a couple of inches all the way around, leaving a seam allowance at the tip of the next tier of squares. That will put the opposite color on the edges, so you might change your mind about the border color.

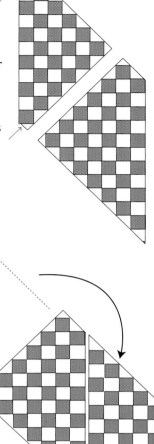

SEWING TIP

Add the borders carefully because the edges of the quilt top are now on the bias. To avoid stretching, pin the borders in place while the quilt is lying flat.

6 Add any outer borders and finish the quilt as desired. For tips on completing your quilt, see Chapter 2.

MAKING DANCING SQUARES FROM OTHER SIZES OF CHECKERBOARDS

Any pieced Checkerboard can be turned on the diagonal if there are an even number of squares in the long direction. But surprising things can happen. For example, if you are making a scrap quilt, the color arrangement will be harder to predict. You'll probably end up with the same colors next to each other diagonally when you sew the edges together, even if you've tried to avoid that in the rest of the quilt.

Your quilt may change its shape after it's turned. If your Checkerboard was square to start with, it will turn out long and skinny after it's been turned. If it was long and skinny to start with, it will turn out square. If it was a fat rectangle, it will turn into another size of fat rectangle.

Here's what happens to the number of dark squares in a Checkerboard after it has been turned. If the Checkerboard had 12 squares the long way, the Dancing Squares will have 6 squares on point the short way. If the Checkerboard had 8 squares the short way, the Dancing Squares will have 8 dark squares on point the long way.

The table below gives the dimensions of Dancing Square Quilt tops from Checkerboards made of strips of four different widths. The measurement in parentheses is the diagonal measurement of the squares after seams.

David's quilt on page 26 has Dancing Squares in the border too—made a different way so the tips of the squares weren't lost in the seams. Although this method is not included here, see page 96 if you would like to order instructions. ★

DANCING SQUARES

Checkerboard Squares (before turning)	Dancing Squares (on point)	APPROXIMATE SIZE OF QUILT WITHOUT BORDERS			
		3½" Strips (4½" diagonal)	4" Strips (scant 5" diagonal)	4½" Strips (5⅝" diagonal)	5" Strips (6¼" diagonal)
6 × 8	4 × 6	17 × 25"	20 × 30"	22 × 34"	25 × 37"
6 × 10	5 × 6	21 × 25"	25 × 30"	28 × 34"	31 × 37"
8 × 10	5 × 8	21 × 34"	25 × 40"	28 × 45"	31 × 50"
8 × 12	6 × 8	25 × 34"	30 × 40"	34 × 45"	37 × 50"
10 × 12	6 × 10	25 × 42"	30 × 50"	34 × 56"	37 × 62"
10 × 14	7 × 10	30 × 42"	35 × 50"	40 × 56"	44 × 62"
12 × 14	7 × 12	30 × 51"	35 × 60"	40 × 67"	44 × 75"

Magic Triangles

Squares are nice, but they just sort of sit there. Squares on point start dancing, but the real magic is when the squares turn into triangles. With triangles you can create all kinds of wonderful blocks like Birds, Flowers, Fish, Stars, Rockets, and Boats.

STRIP-PIECING TRIANGLES

Look at this Dancing Squares Quilt. See how it could be cut apart into strips of triangles?

These strips can be sewn to other strips so that when you finish cutting out your triangles, they are already sewn to other triangles and squares.

It's an assembly-line method for making lots of blocks at one time, very efficient and versatile, when you are used to it.

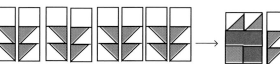

We have two ways of strip-piecing triangles, the original Fast Patch Checkerboard method I developed in 1983 and the Fast Patch Two-Square method we began using in 1995.

FAST PATCH CHECKERBOARD METHOD

This is the method I used in *Fast Patch: A Treasury of Strip Quilt Projects* and *Scrap Quilts Using Fast Patch.* There are no templates, no small pieces to cut, and no short seams to sew or press. Change the size of strips to make larger or smaller blocks. Change the number of strips to make more or fewer blocks. You can use any size of strips to make your Checkerboard, as long as it is four times as long as it is wide, plus 1" for squaring up and allowing for errors.

Use this method if you are used to it and don't feel ready to tackle a new method, if you aren't fussy about the grain of the fabric, and if you like to use long, narrow pieces of fabric.

Sizes of Strips and Triangles

This table shows the most useful sizes of triangles you can make with this technique.

TRIANGLES FROM THE CHECKERBOARD METHOD

Size of Strips	Base of Finished Triangles (APPROXIMATE)
3 × 13"	1 1/4"
4 × 17"	1 7/8 or 2"
5 × 21"	2 5/8"
6 × 25"	3 1/8"

Turning a Square Checkerboard for Triangles

A 4 × 4 Checkerboard, like the one you made in Chapter 2, is the most useful size for this method. Here's how to turn it into triangles.

1 Cut the Checkerboard in half diagonally. So your project will match our example, cut through the light squares first.

2 Sew the pieces back together again, as shown. Look at the magnified area of the diagram. The point of the triangle will be 1/4" from the edge because of the way the seam allowance works.

3 Cut diagonally again. Start your second cut right at the tip of the triangle (shown as a red line).

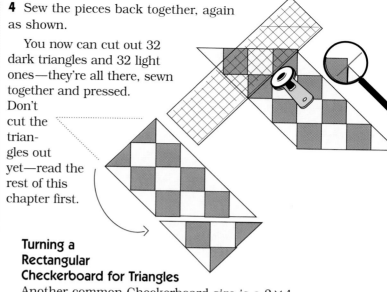

4 Sew the pieces back together, again as shown.

You now can cut out 32 dark triangles and 32 light ones—they're all there, sewn together and pressed. Don't cut the triangles out yet—read the rest of this chapter first.

Turning a Rectangular Checkerboard for Triangles

Another common Checkerboard size is a 2 × 4 rectangle made from one dark strip and one light strip. After turning it, you can cut out 16 dark and 16 light triangles.

1 Cut through any corner. Notice what happens at the edge. You'll cut a 1/4" piece off the next square, because of the way the seam allowances work. Just pull it off when it gets in your way.

2 Sew the triangle you just cut off to the other end of the rectangle, as shown. Again, notice what happens with the seam allowance (at the red dot).

3 Make the second cut at the tip of the triangle, as shown.

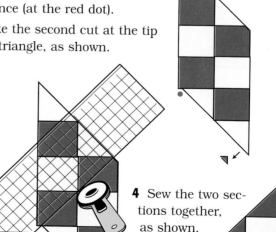

4 Sew the two sections together, as shown.

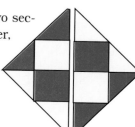

These two Checkerboards—the 4 × 4 and the 2 × 4—are the only types you'll need for this book. Whether you use a large or small Checkerboard, you will cut it apart into strips of triangles, as shown. But don't cut yet—you may need to draw some special guidelines first (see page 38).

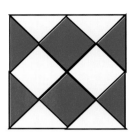

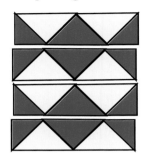

Triangles made from 4" × 17" strips are the most useful size. However, you can make tiny triangles from 3" × 13" strips to use in the Nature blocks shown in Chapter 6, and you can make huge triangles from 7" × 29" strips to use for the sails of Betsy's Boats (described later in this chapter).

Note that when you use the Fast Patch Checkerboard method to make triangles, the grain of some of the fabric in your finished

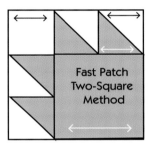

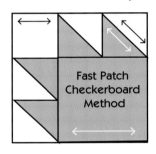

blocks won't run in the traditional direction.

This isn't a problem for everyday quilts. In fact, it's easier to line up the final seams since there is extra stretch in the edges of the triangles.

FAST PATCH TWO-SQUARE METHOD

Use the Two-Square method if you are ready for new ideas, if you want to have the grain of the fabric running in the traditional position, or you want to use squarish pieces of fabric, not long ones. This method is related to Grandma's Secret (page 30), but this is not quite a final quilt block, so we eliminated the seam allowance, thus changing the sizes of the squares we begin with. This is a more precise method, so measure carefully, keeping the cutter blade tight against the ruler, and use consistent seams.

Make the Equivalent of a 4 × 4 Checkerboard from 4" Strips

For this example choose two fabrics, one light and one dark.

1 Cut two 11³/₈" squares—one dark and one light. Spread out the two fabrics, right sides together, and cut both squares at the same time. Keep the squares together for Steps 2 and 3.

2 Cut 4" strips diagonally. First cut through the center, then cut exactly 4" from the center on each side.

Your second cuts will also be 4" to the tips of the triangles, though they won't appear to be.

3 Sew the largest pieces to each other as shown. They are already lined up ready to go. Sew carefully to avoid stretching the bias edges, pinning first, if necessary.

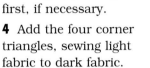

4 Add the four corner triangles, sewing light fabric to dark fabric.

5 Cut the other direction. Lay your ruler from corner to corner.

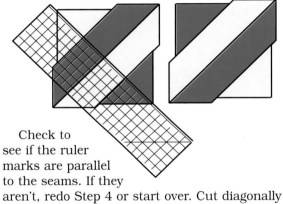

Check to see if the ruler marks are parallel to the seams. If they aren't, redo Step 4 or start over. Cut diagonally down the center. Then cut again 4" away on each side.

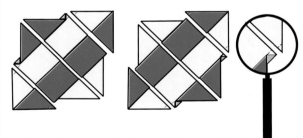

If you have worked carefully and didn't stretch anything, you will cut right at the tip of the triangles in the seam allowance (magnified section). If the cut does not go to this point, check your work. If you think you stretched something, ease it back into shape so your cut will go where it belongs. If you don't notice any mistakes, just do some trimming after you have completed Step 6.

6 Mix up pieces and sew together again. Alternate the lights and darks now. Notice where the seam goes. Also notice what the seams look like with final pressing. (Of course, at this stage it's impossible to press all seams toward the dark.)

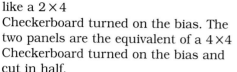

When complete, each panel looks like a 2×4 Checkerboard turned on the bias. The two panels are the equivalent of a 4×4 Checkerboard turned on the bias and cut in half.

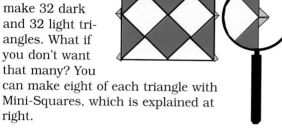

These panels together will make 32 dark and 32 light triangles. What if you don't want that many? You can make eight of each triangle with Mini-Squares, which is explained at right.

Sizes of Squares for the Two-Square Method

You can make triangles the same size as you'd get by using the Checkerboard method. These strips are same width as those listed in "Triangles from the Checkerboard Method" (page 35), but this time they are cut diagonally (Step 2 in "Fast Patch Two-Square Method"). The diagonal measurement of the large squares is equal to the width of four of these strips, rounded up to the next 1/8". The table at right lists the most useful sizes.

COMPLETING THE BLOCKS

You'll complete blocks the same way with both Fast Patch methods of creating Magic Triangles. Here's the general idea.

1 Cut strips of triangles.

2 Sew them to other strips of triangles and to straight strips, which make the squares.

3 Cut off chains of triangles and squares that are already pieced together and pressed.

4 Assemble your final blocks.

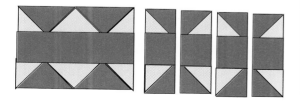

TRIANGLES FROM THE TWO-SQUARE METHOD

Approximate Size of Final Triangles	Size of Squares	Diagonal Measurement	Width of Strips	Size of Mini-Squares
1 1/4"	8 1/2"	12"	3"	4 1/4"
1 7/8"	11 3/8"	16"	4"	5 3/4"
2 5/8"	14 1/4"	20"	5"	7 1/8
3 3/8"	17"	24"	6"	8 1/2"
4 1/4"	20"	28"	7"	10"

MINI-SQUARES FOR JUST A FEW TRIANGLES

The Fast Patch approach is mostly for making a lot of blocks, assembly-line style. But sometimes you want to make only one block, or you need just a few more triangles to replace some that didn't turn out too well. With the Checkerboard method, simply make tiny Checkerboards (2×4 or even 2×2). With the Two-Square method, make Mini-Squares for eight light and eight dark triangles. Here's how.

1 Cut light and dark squares with sides that are half as long as regular Two-Squares.

2 Cut the squares in half diagonally.

3 Sew the squares back together, mixing colors.

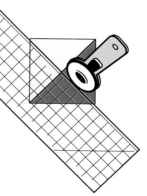

4 Cut the squares diagonally in the opposite direction.

5 Sew the square together again alternating the light and dark fabric.

6 Cut the squares into triangles.

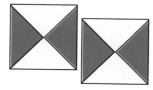
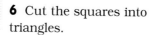
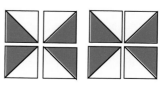

SUCCESS WITH MAGIC TRIANGLES

There are several interesting things to learn for being successful with strip-pieced triangles. We'll discuss them in this section.

MARK CENTERS FOR SOME BLOCKS

When you sew triangle strips to each other, the points must line up. You need the marks in the centers of the triangles in one strip to align with the points of the triangles in the next strip.

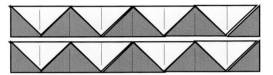

You can do all your marking in a few seconds. Before cutting the panel apart, just draw lines with a regular ball point pen. Disappearing ink isn't necessary because you'll cut here later. If fabric is dark, use a light colored pencil (or cut tiny slashes in the centers).

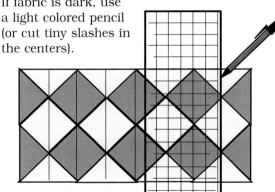

You'll mark one direction and cut the other direction.

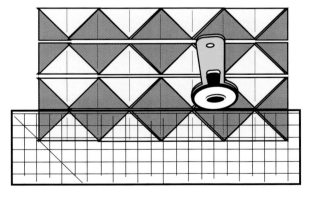

If you forget to mark before you cut the panels, you'll need to individually mark the triangles that will be sewn to other triangles.

CLIP OFF THE MASSES OF SEAMS

You'll get piles of seams at some points. Clip them off with scissors before sewing the strip of triangles to another strip. You can cut into the seam allowance somewhat as you clip off corners. After cutting off what you can, pull off the last bits of cloth, if they bother you (or cut them off at a later step; for example, after sewing the strips to each other and cutting the final chains).

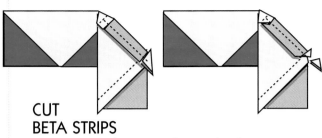

CUT BETA STRIPS

Beta strips—the strips that make the squares—must be the same width as the strips of triangles.

Since you can use wide or narrow strips and since some

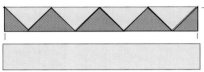

people use slightly wider seams than others, we can't give one simple measurement for those strips, so we call them "Beta strips." Just measure the width of your strips of triangles and cut the strips for the squares to the same width.

What about the length? That depends on how you made your triangle strips.

If you made the triangle strips with the *Fast Patch Checkerboard method*, the edges are stretchy, so have Beta strips exactly the same length (or add only 1/8") and ease the triangle strips to fit. The following table lists some of the most useful sizes.

BETA STRIPS FOR THE CHECKERBOARD METHOD	
Original Strip Size	Typical Size of Beta Strips
3 × 13"	1 5/8 × 13"
4 × 17"	2 3/8 × 19"
5 × 21"	3 1/8 × 25"
6 × 25"	3 7/8 × 31"
7 × 29"	4 5/8 × 37"

If you made triangle strips with the *Fast Patch Two-Square method*, the Beta strips are half as long as that listed in the chart, so you need twice as many. But you can approach the Beta strips differently, since Two-Square triangle strips aren't stretchy. Just use 44"-long strips; sew on all the triangle strips, one after another (sometimes called "tandem piecing"); and then cut them apart. Since the same fabric is usually used in other parts of the project, use any extra lengths for sashing and borders. The width is the only important measurement.

If you used the *Mini-Square method* (page 37), you have only a few triangles, so just cut individual squares instead of using Beta strips.

Beta strips are often sewn to each other rather than to triangles.

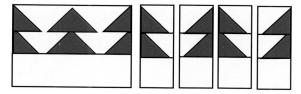

DON'T WORRY ABOUT THE BLUNT POINTS

As you sew strips together, you'll lose the points of the triangles. Those blunt points might disturb you at first, but they are just what you need. You'll cut through the centers of these points and get ¼" seam allowances on each side. When you sew the final chains together, you get all the points back. Do try to keep all the points equally blunt (½" to ⅝" wide).

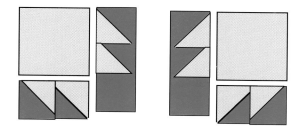

NOTICE THE SLANT OF THE TRIANGLES

Half the triangles will slant one direction and half in the other. As you assemble the blocks, half the blocks will be a mirror image of the other half. You can often turn blocks on their sides to make them all identical.

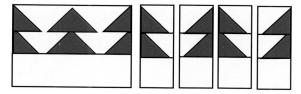

WATCH THE HILLS AND VALLEYS AND THE LIGHTS AND DARKS

When learning a new technique, you may not know whether you've made a mistake or not if your work doesn't look exactly like the diagrams. You might cut your panels slightly differently so the angle of the lines and the placement of the lights and darks don't match the examples

shown in the book. Is that a problem? Usually it isn't, but here's how to check.

This is a panel for the Angel Fish block (Chapter 6) cut into four cross-sections. The loose square at lower left is correct.

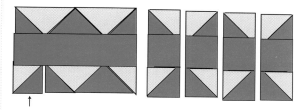

Here's a panel that looks different from the one above. But note that when it is cut into four cross-sections, the chains look the same as the ones above, so it is okay.

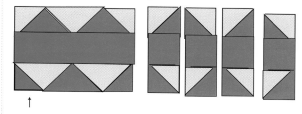

Here's a third panel. This one is not okay for making an Angel Fish block, because the cross-sections are different from the ones shown above.

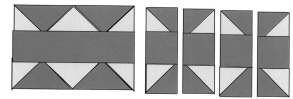

But note that what *isn't* correct for the Angel Fish *is* correct for the Simple Fish (see page 55). There are many ways to combine triangles and squares for the different blocks. Follow the diagrams carefully so you don't get any unhappy surprises. On the other hand, if you goof, you might find that you have invented a new block, or you may find that you've created the pieces of different block shown in this book. So play with your panels and cross-sections a little before you toss anything out.

As a general rule: It usually doesn't matter where the "hills and valleys" are. What counts is whether dark or light edges are against each other.

DESIGN YOUR OWN COLOR SCHEMES

You don't need to copy the colors in the diagrams shown in the book. Here are some guidelines:

◆ Want to switch lights and darks? You can— but maybe not on your first project, unless you have an experienced teacher guiding you and you're willing to make some color sketches that you can follow.

✦ Need more than two colors of triangles? Make a separate Checkerboard (or pair of squares) for each two-color scheme. For the boats described in this chapter, you might have a blue-and-white Checkerboard and a red-and-blue Checkerboard. (If you are using the Two-Square method, you'd have a blue and white squares combination as well as a blue and red squares set.)

✦ Want a scrap look? For a large project, you can use lots of different colors of strips (or squares) and mix up the parts.

Now that you know how to make Magic Triangles you can create many different kinds of pieced blocks. Try out these strip-piecing triangles to make the boats shown in the rest of this chapter. The blocks shown in Chapter 6 also use Magic Triangles, as do some of the blocks in Chapter 7.

A Picture Block Kids Can Make

Children often want to make their own patchwork pictures (especially if they've seen you doing it). But they probably can't sew accurately enough to make most of these kinds of blocks.

Betsy's Boat is one of the best blocks for kids, because it is so forgiving. There are no seams to line up, and it doesn't matter how much sky shows between the sails and boat. If the parts don't match, it's easy to widen seams and trim edges (both of which are more fun than picking out seams).

If the blocks are all sewn together, you can still make the following adjustments yourself—after your FLP has gone to bed, if that's best.

If the bottom is too large:

Trim off parts, as shown.

Or widen these seams and trim off the bottom.

If the top is too large:

Widen this seam and trim off the sides.

Or cut off the bottom of the sails and sky extension. Add a new strip of sky fabric or just have the sails sitting right on top of the boat with no sky showing.

If you want the block to be perfectly square (it doesn't need to be), use a wider or narrower water strip or trim off some of the water.

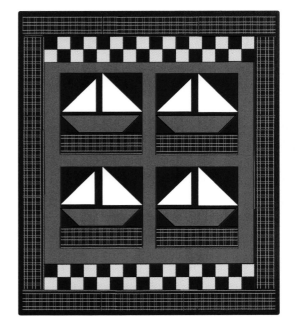

BETSY'S BOATS

Use the Mini-Square method (page 37) to make four of these quick little boats for a nice wallhanging, 22" square (or about 22" × 31" if you add the Checkerboard borders). The blocks are about 7" square. For our example, we'll use blue, white, red, and plaid fabrics, but you can use other colors.

FABRIC NEEDED

✦ ¼ yard (or fat quarter) of white fabric for the sails.

✦ ¼ yard (or fat quarter) of red fabric for the boats and sashing.

✦ ⅓ yard of blue fabric for the background and Checkerboard border.

✦ ⅓ yard of plaid fabric for the water and outside border.

✦ Scraps of tan fabric for the Checkerboard border (or use leftover white fabric).

✦ About ⅓ yard of each additional border fabric.

✦ Binding fabric, backing fabric and batting; the amount needed depends on the width of your borders (see Chapter 2).

MAKING THE QUILT TOP

1 Cut one blue and one white square, each 8½" square.

2 Cut and sew as shown under "Mini-Squares for Just a Few Triangles" on page 37.

3 Make the sails.

a Cut each mini-set into fourths, as shown.

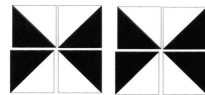

b Trim ½" off the light edge of half the triangles, as shown.

c Cut a 1" × 44" strip of blue fabric, and sew the trimmed edges of those four triangles to this strip (you will use the remaining blue strip in just a minute).

Press and cut apart.

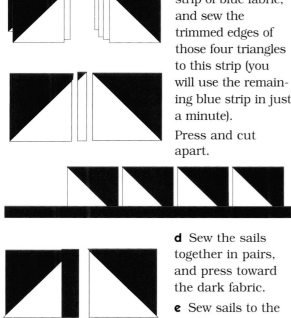

d Sew the sails together in pairs, and press toward the dark fabric.

e Sew sails to the remaining long blue strip, as shown.

If you run short of the blue strip, cut one more 1" × 8" strip from remnants. Cut apart the sets and press.

4 Cut one red and one blue square, each 5¾" square. Again, cut and sew as shown under "Mini-Squares for Just a Few Triangles."

5 Make the bottoms of the boats.

a Cut each mini-set apart, making eight sets of triangles.

b Cut four 2½" × 3½" pieces of red fabric. Adjust the size of these pieces to

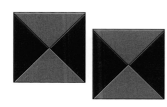

match the red triangles, if necessary, and assemble the boat bottoms as shown.

6 Assemble the tops and bottoms of boat. If they don't match see the sidebar on page 40.

7 Cut a 2" × 24" strip of plaid fabric for the "water." You can make this strip any other desired width. Tandem piece the boats to this strip, and cut them apart.

8 Add 2"-wide red sashing strips and inner borders, referring to the quilt diagram on page 40.

9 Make the Checkerboard borders (optional).

a Cut two 1¾" × 34" strips of blue fabric and two 1¾" × 34" strips of tan fabric. Feel free to use any other colors.

b Sew the strips together in pairs; press. Cut each into sixteen 1¾"-wide cross-sections.

c Sew enough of the cross-sections back together to make two long Checkerboards of the same length as the red border. Doesn't come out even? Trim the side borders down or add additional side borders of another color.

10 Add any final borders and finish the quilt as desired. For tips on assembling and finishing your quilt, see Chapter 2.

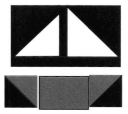

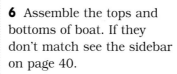

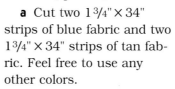

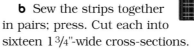

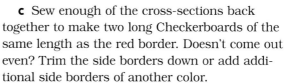

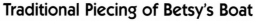

Traditional Piecing of Betsy's Boat

If you want to make only one block, you can use the templates found in the Appendix. Because these templates were designed for the Nature blocks, your boat will not turn out exactly like the Betsy's Boat blocks shown here (or like the boat block in Chapter 7). Here's how to adjust the sky and water strips to fit the templates.

For a 5" Block

Templates: Use the small size, on page 95.

Sky between the sails: ⅞" × 3".

Sky below the sails: ⅞" × 5½".

Water: 1½" × 5½".

For a 7½" Block

Templates: Use the regular size, on page 94.

Sky between the sails: 1" × 4½".

Sky below the sails: 1" × 8".

Water: 2" × 8".

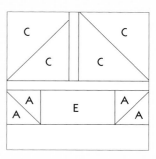

Nona Howell of Fall Creek, Oregon, lined this big, thick Betsy's Boats Quilt with dark blue flannel. Her three-year-old nephew Alex (of Pittsburgh, Pennsylvania) is the lucky recipient of this warm quilt.

BETSY'S BOAT BLOCKS, ASSEMBLY-LINE STYLE

Here's how to make eight 7" blocks using the Checkerboard method and sixteen 7" blocks using the Two-Square method.

Be sure to read through the detailed directions for Betsy's Boats (page 40) before beginning the assembly-line construction outlined here. Use the following table to determine the amount of fabric you'll need. The amount of binding and backing fabric depends on how you set your blocks and the number and width of your borders. See Chapter 2 for more information.

FABRIC FOR ASSEMBLY-LINE BOATS

Element	Checkerboard Method	Two-Square Method
Sails	3/8 yard	1/2 yard
Boats	1/4 yard	1/2 yard
Sky	1/2 yard	2/3 yard
Water	1/4 yard	1/2 yard

GETTING READY

Make panels of uncut Magic Triangles, using whichever method you prefer. Follow the steps outlined at the beginning of this chapter to create the panels. Here are the strip and square sizes you should begin with.

CHECKERBOARD METHOD

Sails: Make a 2 × 4 Checkerboard from one 6" × 25" strip of sail fabric and one 6" × 25" strip of sky fabric.

Boat: Make a 2 × 4 Checkerboard from one 4" × 17" strip of boat fabric and one 4" × 17" strip of sky fabric.

Other pieces to cut: Three 1" × 44" strips of sky fabric, two 3 1/2" × 10" pieces of boat fabric, and two 2" × 44" strips of water fabric.

TWO-SQUARE METHOD

Sails: Begin with one 17" square of sail fabric and one 17" square of sky fabric.

Boat: Begin with one 11 3/8" square of boat fabric and one 11 3/8" square of sky fabric.

Other pieces to cut: Five 1" × 44" strips of sky fabric, four 3 1/2" × 10" pieces of boat fabric, and four 2" × 44" strips of water fabric.

MAKING THE BOATS

1 Make the sails.

a Cut the sail and sky panel(s) apart into triangle sets, as shown.

b Cut 1/2" off the light edge of half the triangle sets.

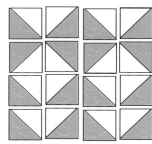

c Replace the strips you cut off with 1" strips of sky fabric. You can tandem piece all the sails to 44"-long strips; then cut the sets apart. Press the sail sets.

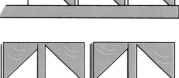

d Tandem piece the sail sets to 1" × 44" strips of sky fabric. Cut the sets apart, and press.

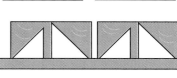

2 Make the bottoms of the boats.

a Cut the boat and sky panel(s) apart as shown.

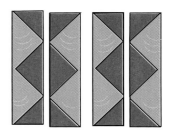

b Sew a 3 1/2" × 10" boat strip between the triangle strips, as shown. If you are changing the size of the boat, adjust the width of this strip so the top and bottom of boat will be the same length.

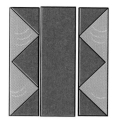

c Cut the boat bottom sets apart as shown. If they don't fit, see page 40.

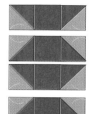

3 Join each sail set to a boat bottom set.

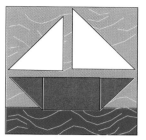

4 Add the water strips (optional) to complete your blocks. Tandem piece the boats to 2" × 44" strips of water fabric.

....

NOTE:

If you use the Two-Square method for the Sailboat blocks, you'll end up with more triangles than you need for the eight blocks. Save the extras and use them for another project.

Betsy's Boats in Other Sizes

One advantage of Fast Patch is the ability to change sizes of blocks by changing the size of the original strips or squares. But with Betsy's Boats, the sails and boat use different sizes of triangles, so use the following lists to help you make the blocks in different sizes. Follow the directions under "Making the Boats" on page 42 to complete your blocks.

MINIATURE—ABOUT 4" SQUARE

Checkerboard Method for 8 Boats

Sails: Make a 2 × 4 Checkerboard from one 4" × 17" strip each of sail fabric and sky fabric.

Boat: Make a 2 × 4 Checkerboard from one 3" × 13" strip each of boat fabric and sky fabric.

Other pieces to cut: Two 1" × 44" strips of sky fabric, two 2" × 6 3/4" pieces of boat fabric, and one 1 1/2" × 44" strip of water fabric.

Two-Square Method

Sails: Begin with one 11 3/8" square each of sail fabric and sky fabric.

Boat: Begin with one 8 1/2" square each of boat fabric and sky fabric.

Other pieces to cut: Three 1" × 44" strips of sky fabric, four 2" × 6 3/4" pieces of boat fabric, and two 1 1/2" × 44" strips of water fabric.

EXTRA-LARGE—ABOUT 9" SQUARE

Note: For extra-large Betsy's Boat blocks, trim off 3/4" from the light edge of half the triangle sets in Step 1b (page 42).

Checkerboard Method for 8 Boats

Sails: Make a 2 × 4 Checkerboard from one 7" × 29" strip each of sail fabric and sky fabric.

Boat: Make a 2 × 4 Checkerboard from one 4" × 17" strip each of boat fabric and sky fabric.

Other pieces to cut: Three 1 1/2" × 44" strips of sky fabric, two 5" × 10" pieces of boat fabric, and two 3" × 44" strip of water fabric.

Two-Square Method

Sails: Begin with one 20" square each of sail fabric and sky fabric.

Boat: Begin with one 11 3/8" square each of boat fabric and sky fabric.

Other pieces to cut: Six 1 1/2" × 44" strips of sky fabric, four 5" × 10" pieces of boat fabric, and four 3" × 44" strips of water fabric.

DESIGN TIPS

Once you are familiar with Betsy's Boats, feel free to make any changes you wish. You might want to make the bottom of the boat larger or smaller for design reasons (recalculate the size of the pieces you sew between the front and back triangles, if you do). You can also have boat and sails be the same color, to stand out against a contrasting sky.

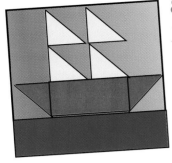

8 MORE SAILBOAT BLOCKS

This traditional Sailboat block appears in my book *Fast Patch: A Treasury of Strip Quilt Projects*. The blocks will be about 7" square. For our boats, we made the sails white, the background teal, the boat red, and the water dark blue. You, of course, can use whatever colors you like.

NOTE:

If you use the Two-Square method for the Sailboat blocks, you'll end up with more triangles than you need for the eight blocks. Save the extras and use them for another project.

GETTING READY

Make Magic Triangle panels, using whichever method you prefer. Mark the centers of the triangles for the sails (see page 38); but it's not necessary for bottom of boat. Here are the strip and square sizes you should begin with.

CHECKERBOARD METHOD

Sails: Make a 4×4 Checkerboard from two 4"×17" strips of sail fabric and two 4"×17" strips of sky fabric.

Boat: Make a 2×4 Checkerboard from one 4"×17" strip of boat fabric and one 4"×17" strip of sky fabric.

TWO-SQUARE METHOD

Sails: Begin with one 11 3/8" square of sail fabric and one 11 3/8" square of sky fabric.

Boat: Begin with one 11 3/8" square of boat fabric and one 11 3/8" square of sky fabric.

OTHER PIECES TO CUT

One Beta strip from the boat fabric, about 2 3/8" × 44".

Two 4 1/4" × 20" strips from the sky fabric.

Two 2 1/2" × 8" strips from the water fabric.

MAKING THE BLOCKS

1 Make the sails.

a Cut strips of triangles from the sail and sky panel.

b Sew the strips together two at a time, matching the points of the triangles at the center marks, and then cut apart, as shown.

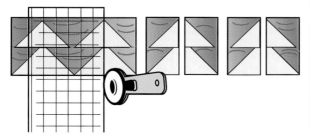

c Choose triangle sets that slant the same way and sew together, as shown. Turn some of the sets, so all the triangles slant in the same direction.

2 Sew the sails to the center bottom of the boats by tandem piecing the sails to the boat fabric Beta strip. Make sure the sails all point in the same direction. Cut the boat sets apart.

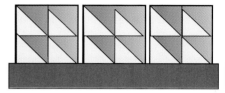

3 Make the fronts and backs of the boats.

a Cut triangle strips from the boat and sky panel; measure the strips.

b Cut the sky strips in half to form 4 pieces the same length as your triangle strips, as shown (adjust as necessary).

c Sew the triangle strips to the background pieces, and then cut the panels into cross-sections, as shown.

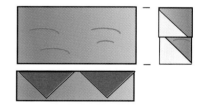

4 Join the sections to make eight boats.

5 Add the water strips to each block, if you wish, completing the eight Sailboat blocks.

CREATIVE IDEAS

Once you've finished your boat blocks, have fun combining them into a creative quilt top. Nona Howell made the quilt shown in the photograph on page 42. Even though her nephew Alex was three when he received this quilt, he will still be using it when he's a teenager because it's big and durable. Notice the unusual arrangement of the boat blocks, which alternate with plain blocks, sashing, and golden stars. The stars were made by simply ending each sashing strip with a gold triangle and putting a gold square in each intersection.

Or use for 16 boat blocks as a border for a simple lighthouse. The lighthouse is quite easy to draw freehand (but see page 96 if you'd like to order instructions).

Sit down with your FLP, your boat blocks, and your fabric stash. Have fun arranging your blocks and coming up with your own special project. ★

CHAPTER SIX

Nine Patch Nature Blocks

This chapter has a colorful collection of birds, butterflies, fish, flowers, and maple leaves to delight your Favorite Little Person. All blocks can be strip-pieced with either method from Chapter 5.

This quilt by Chris Kamon of West Chester, Pennsylvania, is called "Tapico." It includes several different fish blocks, and a variety of buttons was added for the eyes.

To simplify our instructions, we suggest fabric colors for some of the blocks; but, of course, you can use others. Some blocks need special fabrics for the best effect. Songbirds and butterflies are great against background fabric that looks like the sky.

Fish look more like fish if they have a background of variegated blues and greens or something that suggests underwater plants.

Maple Leaf blocks would logically be made from orange-red-brown variegated fabrics.

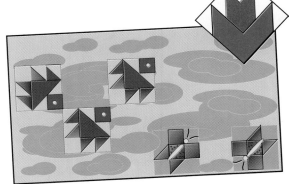

GENERAL INSTRUCTIONS FOR NATURE BLOCKS

All the blocks in the chapter are built up the same way. We'll demonstrate the general idea with four blocks—detailed instructions for these blocks appear a little later.

HOW TO MAKE THE NATURE BLOCKS

1 A square is cut or pieced together. For example:

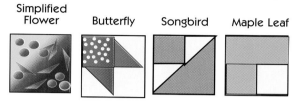

Simplified Flower Butterfly Songbird Maple Leaf

2 A short chain of squares or triangles is then added.

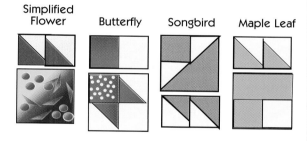

Simplified Flower Butterfly Songbird Maple Leaf

3 A longer chain is added to complete the basic block.

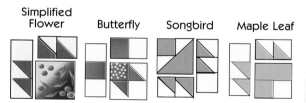

Simplified Flower Butterfly Songbird Maple Leaf

NUMBER OF BLOCKS TO MAKE

We indicate the number of blocks that can be made from one 4 × 4 Checkerboard (or two squares). That is usually 8 blocks but may be 16, if the blocks have fewer triangles. The Tulip block uses two 4 × 4 Checkerboards (or four squares) because two color combinations are needed.

What if you want fewer blocks? With the Checkerboard method, make half as many blocks by making 2 × 4 Checkerboards. If you are using the Two-Square method, start with Mini-Squares (page 37) to make one-fourth as many blocks.

THE TEMPLATE OPTION

You can use templates to piece the Nine Patch Nature blocks, if you prefer. For each type of block, look for the "Traditional Piecing" box. There you will find a list of which templates are used and how many pieces to cut from each fabric. The template patterns themselves are on pages 94 to 95. Two sizes of templates are provided—one set for regular blocks and one set for small blocks.

GETTING ORGANIZED

If you work in the order given here, you'll find that the blocks will come together quickly and easily.

1 For each block, look under "Getting Ready" for information about the fabric, panels, and strips needed to make the block.

2 Make the Fast Patch Magic Triangle panels with either the Checkerboard or the Two-Square method. See the table "Cutting Guide for Nature Blocks" to find the dimensions of the strips or squares. Choose from small or regular blocks.

  a Mark the centers of the triangles, if we say you need to (see page 38).

  b Cut the panels into strips of triangles.

  c Cut the Beta strips. See "Cutting Guide for Nature Blocks" to determine the width of the strip. Cut these strips a full 44" long, unless we say otherwise.

  d Cut any additional strips or pieces listed.

3 Assemble the blocks by following the step-by-step directions and referring to the diagrams.

4 Add embellishments, if desired. Suggestions are listed with each block, if appropriate. But be creative; you and your FLP might be able to think up your own embellishments. (Avoid buttons on quilts for infants.)

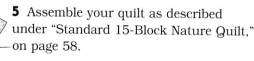

5 Assemble your quilt as described under "Standard 15-Block Nature Quilt," on page 58.

CUTTING GUIDE FOR NATURE BLOCKS

Block Size	Block Dimension	Strips for Checkerboard Method	Squares for Two-Square Method	Width of the Beta Strips to Make Squares	Beta Length
Small	3 3/4"	13" × 13"	8 1/2"	1 3/4"	15"
Regular	5 1/2"	4" × 17"	11 3/8"	2 3/8"	21"

16 BUTTERFLY BLOCKS

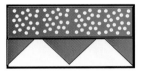

GETTING READY

Fabric: Light for the background, dark solid for the wings and tail, and dark print for the body.

Checkerboard method: One 4 × 4 Checkerboard from light solid and dark solid.

Two-Square method: One square of dark solid and one square of light solid.

Marking: Not necessary.

Beta strips: Four light solid, two dark solid, and one dark print (44" long for regular blocks; 32" long for small blocks); you can make the body from the same fabric as the wings and tail.

MAKING THE BLOCKS

1 Make the first unit.

a Sew half the triangle strips to light Beta strips, dark against light. Cut apart, as shown.

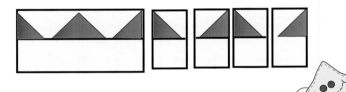

b Sew the remaining triangle strips to the dark print Beta strip, dark against dark. Press toward the plain strips, and cut apart.

 c Piece the units together, as shown.

2 Make short chains. Sew together one dark solid and one light solid Beta strip; press toward the dark fabric. Cut the strips into 16 sets, Beta width.

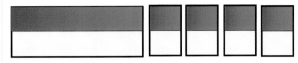

3 Make long chains. Sew together two light solid and one dark solid Beta strip, as shown; press toward the dark fabric. Cut the strips into 16 sets, Beta width.

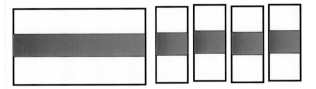

4 Assemble the blocks as shown.

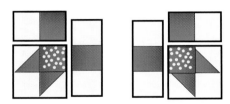

 5 Embellish your Butterfly blocks to get the look you and your FLP want. A large button can be used for the Butterfly's head, or it can be appliquéd or embroidered. The antennae can be embroidered or painted with fabric paint. The body can be appliquéd (you could make the head and body one piece).

Traditional Piecing of Butterflies

(See templates on pages 94–95.)

A triangles: 32 dark solid; 32 light solid.

B squares: 32 dark solid; 64 light solid; 16 dark print.

Note: If you want the body, wings, and tail of the butterfly to be the same color, cut 48 dark solid B squares. Or cut all the dark triangles and squares from the same print.

16 TULIP BLOCKS

GETTING READY

Fabric: White for the background, rose for the flower, and green for the leaves.

Checkerboard method: One 4 × 4 Checkerboard from rose and white; one 4 × 4 Checkerboard from green and white.

Two-Square method: One square of rose with one of white; one square of green with one of white.

Marking: Not necessary.

Beta strips: One rose, one white, and one green.

Other pieces to cut: After measuring to fit in Step 3, one double–Beta width strip of green.

MAKING THE BLOCKS

1 Make the first unit from rose and white triangle strips.

a Sew half of the triangle strips to the white Beta strip, dark against dark, as shown. Cut apart.

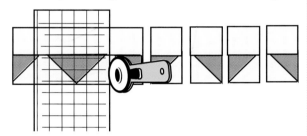

b Sew the remaining triangle strips to the rose Beta strip, dark against dark, as shown. Cut apart.

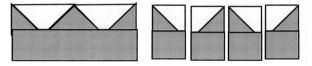

c Piece the units together, as shown.

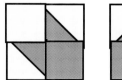

2 Make short chains. Sew half of the green and white triangle strips to the green Beta strip, dark against dark, as shown. Cut apart.

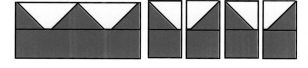

3 Make long chains.

These quilts feature Butterfly and Tulip blocks. Betsy's children Kelly and Joseph Heath (aged six and two, at the time) were photographed at the Springfield (Oregon) Library.

a Measure your rose and white triangle sets. Cut a wide green strip to that measurement, making it long enough to fit the green and white triangle strips.

b Sew the remaining green and white triangle strips to this Beta strip, dark against dark, as shown. Cut apart.

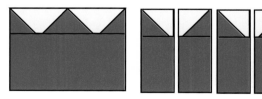

4 Assemble the blocks as shown.

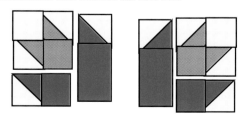

Traditional Piecing of Tulips

(See templates on pages 94–95.)

A triangles: 32 rose; 32 green; 64 white.

B squares: 16 rose; 16 green; 16 white.

E rectangles: 16 green.

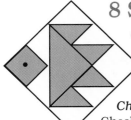

8 SONGBIRD BLOCKS

GETTING READY

Fabric: Light for the background and dark for the fish (or the reverse, if you wish).

Checkerboard method: One 4 × 4 Checkerboard from light and dark.

Two-Square method: One square of light and one square of dark.

Marking: Mark the centers of the triangles.

Beta strips: One light and one dark (21" long for regular blocks; 15" long for small blocks).

Other pieces to cut: One strip ³/₄" wider than Beta width of light; four squares of dark (see Step 1c for size).

MAKING THE BLOCKS

1 Make the first unit.

a Sew the dark Beta strip to the wide light strip, as shown. Cut the strips into 8 sets, Beta width.

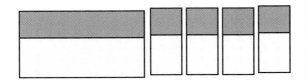

b Reverse half the sets and piece them together, as shown. Then cut the units diagonally at a 45° angle through the light overlap area, as shown, to make the head units. Look at the diagram carefully and watch the angle of your cut—it will not go right to the corners!

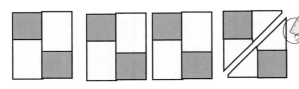

c Measure the longest side of the head units, and cut four dark squares to that size. Then cut the squares in half diagonally (this time going

from corner to corner). Sew the head units to the large dark triangles.

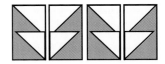

2 Make the short chains. Sew half the triangle strips together, matching the center marks, as shown. Cut apart.

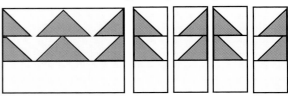

3 Make the long chains. Sew the remaining triangle strips together, matching the center marks, as shown. Add a light Beta strip to the dark side of the triangle strip. Cut apart.

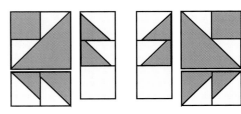

4 Assemble the blocks as shown.

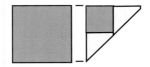

5 Your FLP could pick out buttons for the Songbirds' eyes. You could also embroider the eyes.

Traditional Piecing of Songbirds

(See templates on pages 94–95.)

A triangles: 32 dark; 48 light.

B squares: 8 dark; 8 light.

C triangles: 8 dark.

8 MAPLE LEAF BLOCKS

GETTING READY

Fabric: Light for the background and dark for the leaf (you can use two or three closely related orange-red fabrics instead of making all the parts the same color).

Checkerboard method: One 4 × 4 Checkerboard from light and dark.

Two-Square method: One square of light and one square of dark.

Marking: Mark the centers of the triangles.

Beta strips: Two light and one dark, 21" long (15"), for small blocks, one dark 44" long.

MAKING THE BLOCKS

1 Make the first unit.

a Sew one dark and one light short Beta strip together, as shown. Press toward the dark fabric, and cut into 8 sets, Beta width. Save the remaining light Beta strip for Step 3.

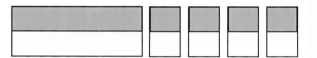

b Sew the sets to the long dark Beta strip, as shown. Cut apart.

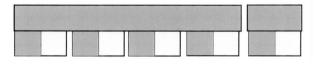

2 Make the short chains. Sew half the triangle strips together in pairs, matching the center of the triangles, as shown. Cut apart.

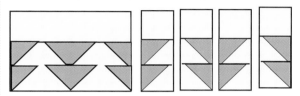

3 Make the long chains. Sew the remaining triangle strips together, matching the center of the triangles, as shown. Add the light Beta strip to the dark side of the triangles, as shown. Press toward the plain strip, and cut apart.

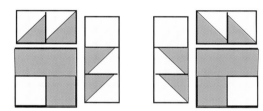

4 Assemble the blocks as shown.

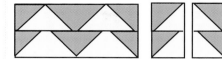

5 Your FLP can paint on the stems, using fabric paint. Or you could embroider or appliqué the stems.

Traditional Piecing of Maple Leaves

(See templates on pages 94–95.)

A triangles: 32 dark; 32 light.

B squares: 8 dark; 16 light.

E rectangles: 8 dark.

Note: If you want a scrappy look, substitute two B squares for each rectangle, giving a total of 24 squares of different

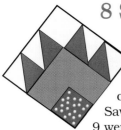

8 SAWTOOTH FLOWER BLOCKS

These blocks are assembled just like Maple Leaf blocks, but by using a different fabric and color combination, you create flowers. The Sawtooth Flower blocks shown on page 9 were set on point.

GETTING READY

Fabric: White for the background, red for the petals, purple for the flower's middle, and print for the flower's center.

Checkerboard method: One 4 × 4 Checkerboard from white and red.

Two-Square method: One square of white and one square of red.

Marking: Mark the centers of the triangles.

Beta strips: One white, one purple, and one print (21" long) for regular blocks; one white, one purple, and one print (15" long) for small blocks; one purple (44" long) for both blocks.

MAKING THE BLOCKS

1 Make the first unit.

a Sew the short print and purple Beta strips together, as shown. Press in either direction, and cut into 8 sets, Beta width.

b Sew these sets to the long purple Beta strip. Cut apart.

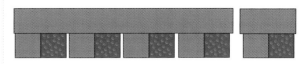

2 Make the short chains. Sew half of the red and white triangle strips together in pairs, as shown. Cut apart.

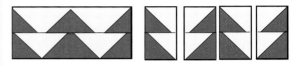

3 Make the long chains. Sew the remaining triangle strips together; then add the white Beta strip to the red side of the triangle strips, as shown. Cut apart.

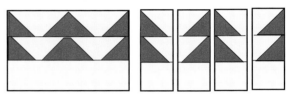

4 Assemble the blocks as shown.

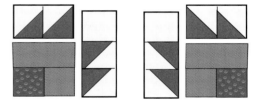

Traditional Piecing of Sawtooth Flowers

(See templates on pages 94–95.)

A triangles: 32 red; 32 white.

B squares: 8 white; 8 print; eight purple.

E rectangles: 8 purple.

8 SIMPLIFIED FLOWER BLOCKS

These blocks are best made on a small scale, because of the large plain square at the base of the flower. This square should be made from an interesting graphic print fabric or embellished with embroidery.

GETTING READY

Fabric: Light for the background, dark solid for the petals, dark print for the flower's base.

Checkerboard method: One 4×4 Checkerboard from light solid and dark solid.

Two-Square method: One square of light solid and one square of dark solid.

Marking: Mark the centers of the triangles.

Beta strips: One light solid (21" long; 15" long for small blocks).

Other pieces to cut: Eight squares of dark print (see Step 3 for details and size).

MAKING THE BLOCKS

1 Make the short chains. Sew half the triangle strips together in pairs, as shown. Cut apart.

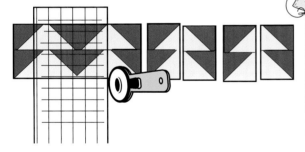

2 Make the long chains. Sew the remaining triangle strips together in pairs, as shown. Add the light solid Beta strip, light against dark, as shown, and press toward the plain strip. Cut apart.

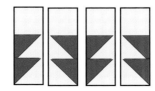

3 Cut out the large squares.

a If using a large print, select just the right pieces of fabric. Lay out the triangle sets from Steps 1 and 2 on the print fabric. Move them around to find 8 sections of the fabric that will look nice with the triangle sets. Your FLP can easily help at this stage.

b Measure the short triangle sets, and cut the 8 print squares to that size.

 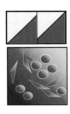 

4 Assemble the blocks as shown.

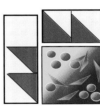

5 Your FLP can embellish the flowers with painted stamens and pistils, if your large squares are rather plain.

Or you could embroider them. The Spring Garden wall quilt includes a pattern (see page 96 for ordering information).

Traditional Piecing of Simplified Sawtooth Flowers

(See templates on pages 94–95.)

A triangles: 32 dark solid; 32 light solid.

B squares: 8 light solid.

D squares: 8 dark print.

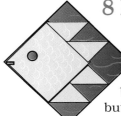

8 BUTTERFLY FISH BLOCKS

These blocks are constructed just like the Simplified Flower blocks. Using different colors, turning the blocks on their side, and adding a button eye make a big difference!

GETTING READY

Fabric: Dark for the background and light for the fish (or the reverse, if you wish).

Checkerboard method: One 4 × 4 Checkerboard from dark and light.

Two-Square method: One square of dark and one square of light.

Marking: Mark the centers of the triangles.

Beta strips: One dark.

Other pieces to cut: Eight squares of light (see Step 2 for size).

MAKING THE BLOCKS

1 Make the short chains. Sew half of the triangle strips together in pairs, as shown. Cut apart.

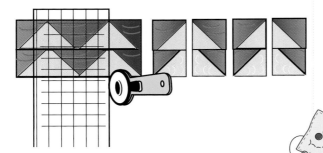

2 Cut out the large squares. Measure the triangle sets you made in Step 1. Cut eight light squares to that size.

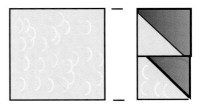

3 Make the long chains. Sew the remaining triangle strips together in pairs, as shown. Then add the dark Beta strip to the light edge of the triangle strip; press toward the plain strip. Cut apart.

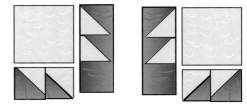

4 Assemble the blocks as shown.

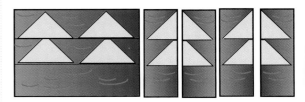

5 Sew on buttons or beads for eyes and embroider a mouth. In the water (dark) area in front of the fish, add buttons to suggest bubbles. Ask your FLP if she would like to sew on the buttons.

Traditional Piecing of Butterfly Fish

(See templates on pages 94–95.)

A triangles: 32 light; 32 dark.

B squares: 8 dark.

D squares: 8 light.

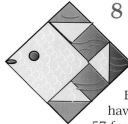

8 SIMPLE FISH BLOCKS

There are fewer triangles to line up when making this fish, so it's easier than the Butterfly Fish. Note that you'll have leftover triangles. See page 57 for a fun way to use them.

GETTING READY

Fabric: Dark for the background and light for the fish (or the reverse, if you wish).

Checkerboard method: One 4 × 4 Checkerboard from dark and light.

Two-Square method: One square of dark and one square of light.

Marking: Optional.

Beta strips: One dark, 44" long.

Other pieces to cut: Eight squares of light (see Step 2 for size).

MAKING THE BLOCKS

1 Make the short chains. Sew a triangle strip to the dark Beta strip, dark against light, as shown. Cut apart. Save the remaining length of Beta strip for Step 3.

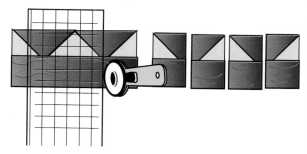

2 Cut the large squares. Measure the short triangle sets you made in Step 1. Cut eight light squares to that size.

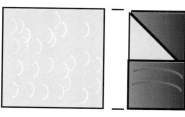

3 Make the long chains. Sew triangle strips to both sides of the remaining length of the Beta strip, dark against light, as shown. Make sure the triangles on both strips line up with each other. Cut straight through the centers of the triangles, as shown.

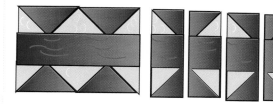

4 Assemble the blocks as shown.

5 As with the Butterfly Fish, sew on buttons or beads for eyes and bubbles, and embroider a mouth if you wish. Ask your FLP if he has any ideas for embellishing the fish, such as drawing scales.

Traditional Piecing of Simple Fish

(See templates on pages 94–95.)

A triangles: 24 light; 24 dark.

B squares: 16 dark.

D squares: 8 light.

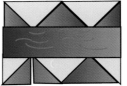

8 ANGEL FISH BLOCKS

These blocks are much like the Simple Fish, but the triangles are turned a different way. It would be easy to make some of both—how you arrange the triangles in Step 3 is the key. Read through this step completely *before* you begin to cut. Note that you'll have leftover triangles. See page 54 for a fun way to use them.

GETTING READY

Fabric: Dark for the background and light for the fish (or the reverse, if you wish).

Checkerboard method: One 4×4 Checkerboard from dark and light.

Two-Square method: One square of dark and one square of light.

Marking: Optional.

Beta strips: One dark; 44" long.

Other pieces to cut: Eight squares of light (see Step 2 for size).

MAKING THE BLOCKS

1 Make the short chains. Sew a triangle strip to the dark Beta strip, dark against dark, as shown. Save the remaining length of Beta strip for Step 3.

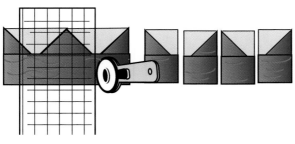

2 Cut out the large squares. Measure the triangle sets you made in Step 1. Cut 8 light squares to that size.

3 Make the long chains. Sew a triangle strip to the remaining length of the Beta strip, dark against dark, as shown.

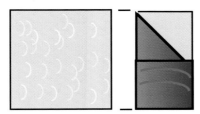

4 Now add a second strip of triangles to the other side, light against dark—*but study the diagram and read through this step* to be sure you have positioned the second triangle strip correctly.

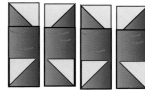

5 To make the second strip come out right, you need to make a small adjustment. Note that the lower left triangle set in the diagram above is not attached to the rest of the triangle strip. It was cut from the other end of the strip to be used here. (Just sew it to the Beta strip and let it flap; don't piece it to the rest of the triangle strip. In fact, you can sew that triangle set on after cutting apart the chains.)

6 The triangles still need to line up accurately so you can make a straight cut through the centers. Press toward the center strip, and cut the panel apart, as shown above.

7 Assemble the blocks as shown.

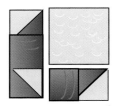

8 Embellish the fish with buttons, beads, or embroidery. Your FLP will probably have definite ideas about how she wants her fish to look—just ask!

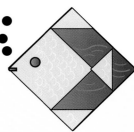

Traditional Piecing of Angel Fish

(See templates on pages 94–95.)

A triangles: 24 dark; 24 light.

B squares: 16 dark.

D squares: 8 light.

USING THE LEFTOVERS: 8 FISH-IN-A-FLASH

Here's a fun way to use a strip or two of leftover triangles, in any colors. A child can assemble these blocks because there's just one seam to line up and the blocks can be trimmed after they're made. (Reverse the darks and lights if that gives a better fish and water effect.) Use the "Getting Ready" section if you don't have any leftover triangle and Beta strips.

The directions here are for eight fish; adjust the length of the wide and regular Beta strips to fit how ever many triangle sets you have on hand. The triangles might be in one long strip or two shorter strips—or you can attach single triangles, if that's what you have to work with.

GETTING READY

Fabric: Dark for the background and light for the fish (or the reverse, if you wish).

Checkerboard method: One 2 × 4 Checkerboard from dark and light.

Two-Square method: One Mini-Square (page 37) of dark and one of light.

Marking: Not necessary

Other pieces to cut: See the step-by-step directions.

MAKING THE BLOCKS

1 Make the first unit.

a Cut a 4 1/2" × 21" strip of dark (2 3/4" × 13" for small blocks) .

b Sew triangle strips to the wide strip, light side against dark side, as shown. Press toward the plain strip, and cut apart as shown.

2 Make the second unit.

a Cut a 4 1/2" × 44" strip of light (2 3/4" × 27" for small blocks).

b Cut a 2 1/2" × 44" strip of dark (1 3/4" × 27" for small blocks).

c Sew the two strips together.

d Press toward the darker fabric, and cut eight 2 1/2" cross-sections (1 3/4" for small blocks), as shown.

....

CUTTING TIP

The strips cut in Step 2 are a bit larger than normal, because it's so easy to trim these blocks down. You can make them even wider if you're in a hurry or if the blocks are being created by a beginner or a child.

3 Assemble the blocks as shown.

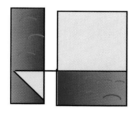 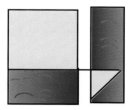

4 Trim off any surplus to square up the block.

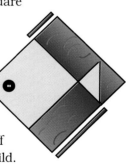

5 Embellish the fish as desired. Try using a button for the eye—most kids can sew on a button. Just be careful to reinforce the button so it can't be pulled off and swallowed by a young child.

Traditional Piecing of Fish-in-a-Flash

(See templates on pages 94–95.)

A triangles: 8 light; 8 dark.

D squares: 8 light.

E rectangles: 16 dark.

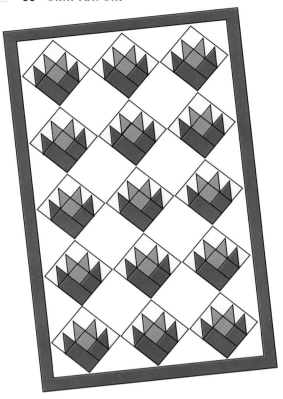

STANDARD 15-BLOCK NATURE QUILT

This standard arrangement is designed for use with the regular size Nature blocks. Use any blocks that you and your FLP like. Note that the exact amount of fabric needed will depend on the specific block(s) you want to make.

Regular blocks make a 24" × 39" baby quilt before the borders (and 37" × 51" if you add a couple of borders). Use small blocks for a 16" × 27" wallhanging before the borders.

FABRIC NEEDED

◆ 1/2 to 2/3 yard of light fabric for the pieced blocks (white in our example).

◆ 1/2 yard of bright fabric (main color) for the pieced blocks (green in our example).

◆ 1/4 to 1/2 yard contrasting fabric (accent color) for the pieced blocks (light blue in our example).

◆ 2/3 yard for the plain blocks and triangles (white in our example).

◆ 1/3 to 1/2 yard for each border fabric.

◆ Binding fabric, backing fabric, and batting; the amount needed depends on the width of your borders (see Chapter 2).

MAKING THE QUILT TOP

1 Make 16 Nine Patch Nature blocks, using the instructions earlier in this chapter. You'll have one extra block—use it for a potholder or to decorate the back of your quilt.

2 Cut the plain squares and triangles.

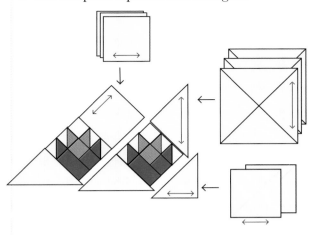

a Cut 10 squares from the white fabric, making them the same size as the patchwork blocks (about 6"). Cut two of these squares in half diagonally to make the four corner triangles.

b Cut three 10" squares from the white fabric. Cut each of these squares in half diagonally in both directions to make 12 edge triangles.

3 Assemble the quilt top. Arrange the rows of patched blocks, plain blocks, and plain triangles, as shown. Sew the rows together, making sure the seams are aligned.

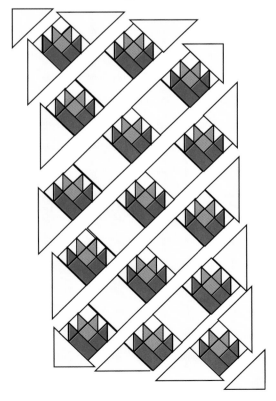

4 Add any borders and finish the quilt as desired. For tips on completing your quilt see Chapter 2.

OTHER SETTINGS AND BORDERS

MORE SETTINGS ON POINT

Most Nine Patch Nature blocks look good set on point alternating with plain blocks. Regular blocks measure 7³/₄" diagonally, and the small blocks measure 5¹/₄" diagonally.

Here are some good arrangements for Nature block quilts.

✦ *Make 16 blocks.* Set the blocks in four rows of four blocks. The regular blocks will yield a 32" square quilt before the borders. Use the smaller blocks to create a 21" to 22" square quilt without the borders.

✦ *Make 24 blocks.* Set the blocks in four rows of six blocks. This quilt top will be about 32" × 47" before the borders (or 21" × 32" if smaller blocks are used).

✦ *Make 24 mixed blocks.* For example, make half-sets of the blocks (using 2 × 4 Checkerboards). Try mixing eight Butter-flies, four Songbirds, eight Tulips, and four Maple Leaf blocks. Then set the blocks in four rows of six blocks. Ask your FLP to help you arrange the blocks to make a quilt that suits her style.

CREATING LEAVES FOR SAWTOOTH FLOWERS

The Sawtooth Flower blocks need to have some sort of leaves added, if nothing more than green sashing to suggest leaves. Here are several possibilities.

You could build up the sashing and leaves Log Cabin block style. Sew all the Sawtooth Flower blocks to the long strips, then cut them apart. Then sew the blocks another strip along a different side.

Once you get the hang of adding the sashing in a Log Cabin style you can set the blocks in all sorts of creative ways. Here are some examples to get your imagination running.

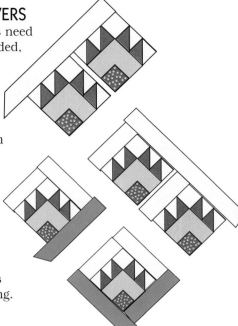

This quilt was made by Betsy for her daughter Hannah—the baby's name and birth date are embroidered in the lower area. The appliquéd basket is surrounded by a Tulip block border. Except for the corner blocks, the quilt was machine quilted.

USING THE BLOCKS FOR BORDERS

The Nature blocks in this chapter can be used for patchwork borders. They would be a great addition to medallion quilts.
Here are some diagrams that will help you see how to assemble these borders. Notice how smaller triangles are used to fill in the corners.

For some quilts, you may want to use solid squares in the corners. Here's how such a quilt top would be put together.

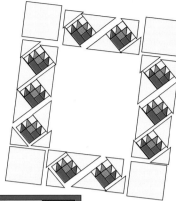

In this example, the leaves of the Sawtooth Flowers were assembled a little differently to create a border design.

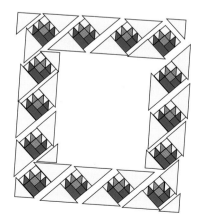

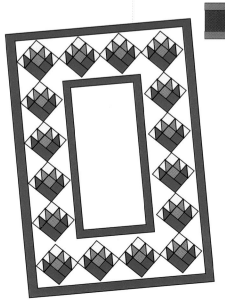

OTHER CREATIVE IDEAS

COMBINING BLOCKS

✦ *Bear's Paw.* Each of these blocks is made up of four corners that are basically Butterfly Fish or Simplified Flowers. The corners are set together with four bars and a center square. Make this block on small scale only. For this version, all the blocks are identical; but you might want to make each block with different fabrics.

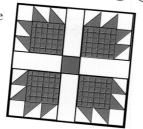
Bear's Paw

✦ *Four-block combinations.* You saw how Bear's Paw was a combination of four small blocks. Other blocks can also be combined (a good way to use leftovers, by the way). Here are some examples:

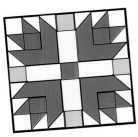
Tulip Blocks

Butterfly Blocks

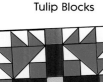

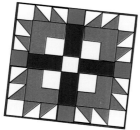
Songbird Blocks
(creates Grandmother's Choice)

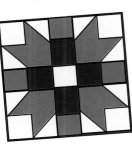
Maple Leaf

✦ *Sister's Choice.* If only the first steps of the Tulip block are used, you get Sister's Choice. This wonderful block was featured in my book *Fast Patch: A Treasury of Strip Quilt Projects,* along with 15 different light and dark combinations for this block and more of a closely related block.

PET BLOCKS

These Pet blocks are also Nine Patch Nature blocks built up of simple squares and triangles. After you practice the Nature blocks in this chapter, you might be able to make up a Pet block easily. If you need instructions, see page 96 for mail order. Ask your FLP to help you choose fabrics to match his favorite pet. Embellish these blocks with buttons and embroidery. Make the birds' beaks and the dogs' and cats' ears from folded pieces of fabric that are sewn into the seams.

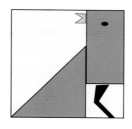
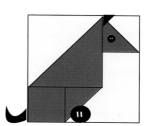

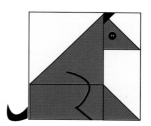
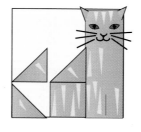
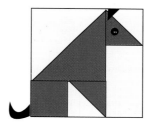
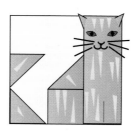
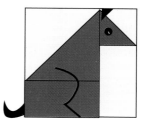
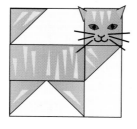
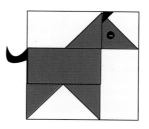

UNIQUE WALLHANGINGS

Here are some ways that the Nature blocks can be mixed together and arranged into one-of-a-kind wallhangings; these are usually made with the small blocks. You and your FLP can have lots of fun arranging these wallhangings with a variety of blocks. If you feel that you need more detailed instructions for creating these types of quilts, see page 96 for mail-order information.

✦ *Medallion Quilts.* You were introduced to medallion quilts in Chapter 3. Here are two that feature Nature blocks. The center design in both quilts uses the four-block combinations shown earlier. The borders were built up of similar blocks, Checkerboards, or other patchwork. The possibilities are endless, so you and your FLP can just make it up as you go along. The photograph on page 63 shows Pam Dittmar's version of a medallion quilt.

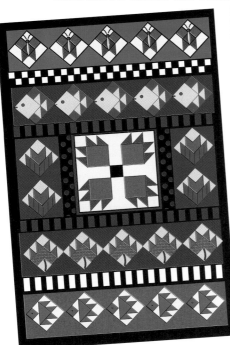

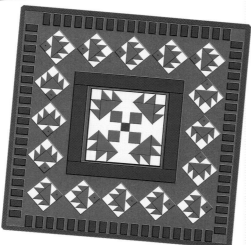

✦ *Flower Bed.* This wallhanging is about 31" × 47". It is made of 14 Sawtooth Flower blocks. Chapter 3 tells you how to set your sashing on point, so you can create the center of this quilt top. The background is basically made up of four big triangles, cut from two 15" squares. If you are using a directional print, be careful to keep the design going the right way. The Tulip border was made in a similar fashion as the Sawtooth Flower border (page 60) was made. Here, the top Tulip border was set upside down for the color effect; you don't need to do it that way (see also the photograph on page 91).

✦ *Betsy's Ocean.* The photograph on page 7 show's Betsy's Ocean Quilt. She used a variety of fish, both regular and small sizes. She embellished some of the fish with button eyes. The marine life at the bottom of the quilt was done with appliqué.

✦ *Spring Garden.* My Spring Garden quilt (see the photo on page 7) is an example of just making up the quilt as you go along and letting what you have made in one part dictate what you add next. The Songbirds and Butterfly blocks are turned in all different directions to make them flitter above the wrought iron fence. I used black backgrounds for the Songbirds and Butterflies so that I could use the same strip-pieced triangles I used for the Simplified Flowers below. The big pink flowers looked a bit too plain on the completed quilt top, so I used metallic thread and tiny beads to make stamens and pistils.

✦ **By the Lake.** This quilt uses Betsy's Boats from Chapter 5 (two would be enough). Here four Butterflies flitter in the sky. You could use Songbirds instead. The quilt also features four Tulip blocks made with a special long stem beneath each. The little yellow butterflies in the flowers are actually a variation of the Tulip block. The trees in the background are nothing more than uncut triangle strips—you lose the points of the triangles as you sew them together, but that adds to the effect. Make an extra-wide seam to lose more of the points, if you'd like.

The medallion quilt was made by Pam Dittmar of Provo, Utah. It features various Nine Patch Nature blocks, including birds, Butterflies, Bear's Paws, and flowers. Betsy made the Bear's Paw Quilt in a six-block arrangement.

✦ **Aquarium.** This quilt uses two different fish blocks. Most of the plants were made from leftover triangle sets—deliberately misalign the triangles for a wobbly, underwater effect. You could also make them from Mini-Squares. Note that the background fabrics suggest water. Look for similar fabrics or prints that show or suggest seashells, castles, shipwrecks, gravel, colored stones, seaweed, etc. Take your FLP with you when you go shopping for fabric. To create the look of an aquarium, use black borders, wide on the top and bottom and narrow at the edges. Put a border of yellow fabric or lamé along the top to suggest the light. ★

CHAPTER SEVEN

The Playroom Quilt

The Playroom Quilt, with its shelves full of colorful books and toys, will take more time to make than the other quilts presented in this book. But this one may become one of your FLP's favorite things, especially if it's personalized with his name and his favorite book titles and toys.

When I made this Playroom Quilt, I placed four Toy blocks on each shelf. Notice that the Dinosaur, Hobby Horse, Doll, and Clown blocks all face toward the center of the quilt.

The blocks for the Playroom Quilt are about 7 1/4" square after seams. If you use 16 blocks, the finished quilt will be about 38"×44". You can arrange the finished blocks in any order you wish. Leave out some of the blocks, use some of the blocks twice, or substitute other blocks from your imagination. Examine the diagrams and photographs and read the "More Ideas" section at the end of this chapter for some suggestions.

You can't do much strip-piecing for this quilt since you'll probably make only one of each block. But you'll be able to make almost all of the blocks with just your 6" ruler and rotary cutter.

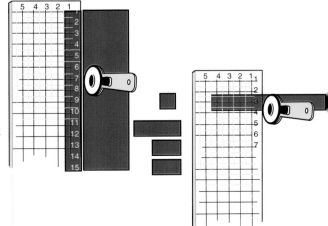

The Doll block does need templates, however, since it's made up of odd pieces; but even that block goes together in a flash with straight-line piecing. You can piece all the blocks in a few hours.

Making creative decisions and adding embellishments can take many more hours. You and your Favorite Little Person can have fun rummaging through your stash of buttons, laces, and trims to choose just what she wants to make her quilt unique.

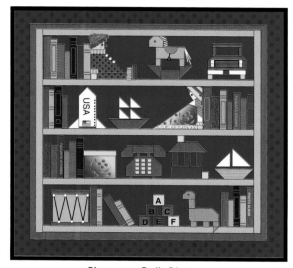

Playroom Quilt Diagram

OVERVIEW OF THE TOY BLOCKS

Here's a list of the Toy blocks along with some of my construction and embellishing notes. Look at the Quilt Diagram (above) and identify each block as you read through the list. Details for making a Playroom Quilt and patterns for the blocks follow this list. The blocks listed first are very quick and easy. As you go down the list, the blocks will require more time and fussing.

BLOCK	NOTES
Box	This is the easiest block. There's no pattern for this block because you can make it in any size needed to fill up extra space. Use an elegant metallic fabric to make a Treasure Box or a cartoon picture to suggest a Jack-in-the-Box with its lid closed. Just cut a rectangle about 4" to 6" wide. Add a lid by sewing a strip of another fabric about 1½" wide across the top. Add background fabric as needed to complete the block.
Standing Books	There's no pattern for this block, either, but we've given you con-

struction diagrams. Books can be any width or height. It's a good idea to make the Book blocks last, when you know what colors and sizes you need to balance your quilt top. Use lots of new fabrics, plus those already used (but don't use the background or sashing color). Add the titles of your FLP's favorite books.

Drum	This is an ideal block for the Playroom Quilt because it is very easy to make and it can be used to "hold up" the book blocks. Although we've provided a block pattern for the Drum, you could make it in any size needed to balance your quilt. Embellish this block with colorful cord and buttons.
Leaning Books	Make one Leaning Book for a block about 4½" wide or make two or more Leaning Books for a bigger block. Again, you can embellish these blocks with book titles or try adding the name of your FLP's favorite game or puzzle.
Building Blocks	The Building Blocks are very easy to make, and they don't need to be perfectly centered. No embellishment is needed, but you might want to add some letters to the sides, as shown in the Quilt Diagram.
Betsy's Boat	Although we gave you detailed instructions for strip-piecing this block in Chapter 5, We've included a pattern of Betsy's Boat just for the Playroom Quilt. Although no embellishment is needed for this block, you could add a star, numbers, or a name.
Rocket	The Rocket block can be narrow (5½" wide), or you can add background fabric on the sides. I added a flag, "USA," and rivets to the rocket in the Quilt Diagram. You could add stars or the name of the rocket—ask your FLP what he wants.
House	I used many colors for the House block in the Quilt Diagram to suggest painted building blocks. You could use a single fabric to imitate wood or use the colors of your FLP's house. No embellishment is needed.

PLANNING AHEAD TIP

Consider embellishing some of the fabric with paint or machine embroidery <u>before</u> cutting out the pieces—for example, to add titles to the Book blocks, to personalize the Car license plate, or to embellish the Rocket. That way you can redo the pieces if you don't get them right the first try. If your FLP is helping you do the embellishment, she will be able to try out several ideas before picking the one she likes.

Sailboat   In Chapter 5, we showed you how to strip-piece multiple Sailboat blocks, but since you'll probably need just one block for this quilt, we have given you a block pattern. Make it in the same colors as the other boat or not. No embellishment is needed, although you could add a name or stars.

Telephone   The Telephone block in the Quilt Diagram is a "touch-tone" phone. You can use buttons, beads, or other embellishments. You might even find a suitable print fabric with $3/8$" squares to suggest the keypad. Another idea is to use buttons in a circle to make a dial phone.

Dinosaur   The Dinosaur block is sure to be a hit with your FLP. Add a button eye. This block can sit on its own base or sit on the shelf, with its tail breaking into the sashing, as shown in the Quilt Diagram.

Car   Although the car in the quilt diagram is plain, you might want to add a steering wheel when piecing the block or embroider one later. Personalize the license plate with the initials of your FLP.

Hobby Horse   Add a saddle and stirrup when piecing. You can embroider a mane and tail and add a button eye later.

Doll   You must piece the Doll block with templates. Add the lace and hat band when piecing, and add the hair, hat ribbon, and eye later.

Clown   The Clown block is easy to piece, but won't look like the one in the Quilt Diagram until you decorate it. Embellishing the Clown may take more time than any other block. Add the ruffles when piecing, and add the eye, nose, cheek, hair, and buttons later.

The full-size block patterns don't show seam allowances, but $1/4$" seam allowances are included in all the calculations.

You can do some of the piecing on a paper foundation with a sew-and-flip technique, if you prefer that method. Make an extra photocopy of each block pattern you plan to piece this way. The Doll block is especially suited to foundation piecing.

FABRIC AND EMBELLISHMENTS

Read through the following lists to get an idea of the amount of fabric and types of embellishments you'll want to have on hand. Since each Playroom Quilt is unique, exact yardages and notions will vary.

FABRIC

+ $3/4$ yard of a dark fabric for the background (a printed solid is okay if there is no obvious design).
+ $1/3$ yard of white for the Rocket and the boats' sails.
+ $1/3$ yard of red for several Toy blocks.
+ $1/2$ yard of a light or medium fabric for sashing (shelves) and the inner border. A lighter shade of the background color will give a good illusion of shelves.
+ $1/4$ yard of a bright color for a narrow accent border, if desired.
+ $1/2$ yard of a printed fabric for the outside borders (a wallpaper-looking fabric works nicely).
+ $1 1/4$ or more yards of a printed fabric for the backing.
+ Batting. Cut it about 2" wider than the quilt top in all directions.
+ $1/3$ yard of a contrasting fabric for the binding.

You'll also need scraps of bright solids, prints, strips, and plaids for the Toy blocks. See "Cutting the Pieces," for details. Remember, although we have suggested colors for the blocks, you can use whatever colors you and your FLP like.

EMBELLISHMENTS

Substitutions can be made for most of the embellishments—use your imagination. We've included embellishment ideas in our block construction directions, so be sure to read them carefully. The photographs and diagrams also show embellishment ideas.

+ Embroidery floss or fabric paint to create details.
+ Iron-on letters and numbers for the Building Blocks and Books—check that they are washable.
+ Flag—embroidered patch about 1" × 1 1/2" or Boy Scout uniform patch.
+ Embroidered stars or hearts, if desired.
+ Middy braid or rattail cording for the Hobby Horse's saddle, the Drum, and the Car's steering wheel.

- Yarn for the Doll, Clown, and Hobby Horse.
- Buttons for the Drum, Hobby Horse, Telephone, Dinosaur, Clown, and Doll (unless the quilt is for a small child who might swallow them).
- Scraps of ribbon, ruffles, rick-rack, and lace for Doll and Clown.

GETTING ORGANIZED

Even messy people can do strip-piecing. You have to be better organized for a project with so many different blocks! It's no fun looking for little pieces of fabric in a jumbled-up mess. You'll do a little cutting, a little sewing, then a lot of cutting and a lot of sewing.

WORKING PAGES

Make photocopies of the full-size block patterns at the end of this chapter to use as "working" pages. As you choose and cut your fabrics, temporarily attach the pieces to these pages to keep them organized until you can sew the blocks. You will also need to photocopy or carefully trace the templates for the Doll block.

FABRIC AND TRIM

To start with, you'll need the background fabric and minimum lengths of most of the other fabrics. If a fabric you want to use is in a 5-yard length, cut off a 1/4- to 1/2-yard piece and put the rest away. Leave the sashing, border, binding, and backing fabrics out of the way.

The only embellishments you need at this stage are cording (for the Car's steering wheel and the Hobby Horse's stirrup) and lace and ruffles (for the Doll and Clown). After all the blocks are made and the materials are cleared away, you can get out your yarn, embroidery floss, and other trims and finish decorating the blocks. Add the buttons after the quilt is almost complete.

YOUR WORK SPACE

Have the following materials within reach at your cutting table.

- Your working pages.
- This book.
- Glue stick to hold the fabric pieces in place temporarily (or pins on a wrist pin cushion).
- Cutting mat and rotary cutter.
- Rulers (6"×12", 6"×24") and grids (6" square, 8" square).
- Fabrics and embellishments for assembling the blocks.
- Something to label the dark fabrics with (Post-It notes, stickers, masking tape).

- A box to hold the scraps you'll use for the Books, Box, or other blocks at a later stage.
- A waste basket.
- An iron and an ironing surface, ideally within reach of both the cutting area and the sewing machine.

ORGANIZING TIP

If your sewing machine isn't close to your cutting table, it's handy to have a small set of cutting tools and an iron there also. A travel iron and piece of cardboard padded with a towel will do.

CUTTING THE PIECES

First, you and your FLP need to choose which blocks you want to make. Note that this quilt will be quicker to make and the design will be more unified if you make several Book blocks and you don't include all of the Toy blocks.

Read "Overview of the Toy Blocks" (page 65), keeping in mind that the blocks listed first will be the quickest to make. Adjust the following cutting and piecing directions, eliminating the blocks you're not going to make.

MAKE MAGIC TRIANGLES

Use the Mini-Square method (page 37) for making Magic Triangles (detailed in Chapter 5).

Red and Background Triangles

Start with one 6 3/8" square *each* of red and background fabric, and complete the triangle panels.

Cut the panels into the following triangle sets:

☐ *For the Hobby Horse:* cut two 2 5/8" squares.

☐ *For the Sailboat:* cut two 2 1/2" squares.

☐ *For the House:* cut two 2 1/2" squares.

Relax—These Blocks Are Friendly

- We suggest colors to use to simplify the instructions, but you can usually substitute other fabrics.
- If you ruin a block or don't want to fuss with decorating a block, just make extra Books, Building Blocks, or Boxes. Or make the quilt smaller.
- If the pieces you have cut don't fit exactly as shown in the pattern, it may not matter. To simplify cutting, we occasionally cut a piece a bit too large, then trim off the excess when the block is finished.
- The exact size of the blocks isn't crucial in this quilt. Many blocks can be trimmed down without any trouble. If blocks turn out different sizes, put all the taller ones together on the same shelf, the shorter ones on another shelf. Add more Books or strips of background fabric to fill in any extra space.

You'll have extra triangle sets. If you wish, cut two more 2 1/2" squares to make the bottom of Betsy's Boat. If you do this, then the two boats will be the same color; we made our boats from different fabrics.

White and Background Triangles

Start with one 9 1/4" square *each* of white and background fabric, and complete your triangle panels.

Cut the panels into the following triangle sets:

☐ *For Betsy's Boat:* cut two 4 1/4" squares. Trim off 1/2" from the white side of one square, as shown by the dashed line.

☐ *For the Rocket:* cut two 2 1/8" squares; cut one 1 7/8" × 3" rectangle (include a 1/4" seam allowance at the top, as shown).

☐ *For the Sailboat:* cut four 2 3/8" squares (from the corners, as shown).

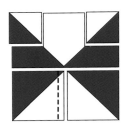
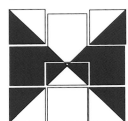

 Ask your FLP to use the glue stick to attach the triangles to their working pages, as shown.

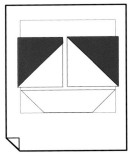
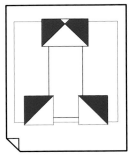

CUT THE REST OF THE FABRIC

Refer to the following cutting lists. You have permission to photocopy these pages to use as a checklist. Cross off any references to blocks you decided not to make. Even if you don't need all the background and red strips, we suggest you go ahead and cut them all anyway. Use the extra lengths for Book blocks and to fill in spaces when you arrange your blocks.

Cut the Background Fabric

You'll need lots of large and small pieces of the background fabric. You can make them fast by cutting long strips and then cutting off smaller pieces. Cut background strips to sizes given in the following chart. The code refers to letters on the block patterns.

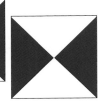

BACKGROUND STRIPS FOR PLAYROOM QUILT

Code*	Number to Cut	Width	Length
A	2	1"	44"
B	2	1 3/4"	44"
C	1	2"	44"
D	1	2 1/2"	44"
E	1	3"	22"
F	1	3 1/2"	22"

Used on block patterns, at back of chapter

Leave these strips out on your cutting mat, doubled with a label of some sort at the fold.

Switch to your 6" × 12" ruler, if you have one. Look at the block patterns. Every space with a code letter needs the background fabric, so cut off pieces in the sizes given. You'll often need two or four pieces the same size, so cut through more than one layer when you can. Do all the background pieces for one block, paste the fabric to your working page, set it aside, then work on another block.

As you cut the pieces, your FLP can touch the glue stick lightly to the paper and stick the fabric in place. Don't use much glue.

Notice that some squares on the block patterns are outlined with dotted lines. Those squares round off the rectangles (page 70). Cut the squares now, but just stick them in the margin of the working pages until you have cut the pieces you'll sew them to.

Also cut the following pieces from the background fabric:

☐ *For the Leaning Books:* cut one 5" × 8" piece.

☐ *For the Hobby Horse:* cut one 1 1/4" square.

☐ *For the Doll:* cut two pieces (use the templates).

Put the leftover background strips in your remnant box to use for Book and Box blocks later. You won't know what sizes of fabric you'll need until you make those blocks.

Cut the Basic-Color Fabrics

Note that measurements for other colors do not appear on the block patterns. Simply cut all the pieces of one color and distribute them to all the working pages that need them; then go on to the next color. If a page becomes so covered with fabric that the paper doesn't show, don't glue on the last little pieces; just lay them on top. When a working page has all the pieces it needs, set it aside.

As you work down these lists, cut Books from each color. Cut strips of fabric any size from 1" to 2" wide and 5" to 7" long. Or put the leftover fabric aside and cut the Books later.

Red Fabric

CUT ONE 1" × 22" STRIP. FROM IT, CUT THE FOLLOWING:

☐ *For the Telephone:* cut two 1" pieces.

☐ *For the Car:* cut one 6 3/4" piece; cut one 5 1/2" piece; cut two 2" pieces; cut two 1 1/2" pieces.

CUT ONE 1 1/8" × 22" STRIP. FROM IT, CUT THE FOLLOWING:

☐ *For the Drum:* cut two 7 1/4" pieces.

☐ *For the Car:* cut one 6 3/4" pieces.

CUT ONE 1 1/4" × 22" STRIP. FROM IT, CUT THE FOLLOWING:

☐ *For the Leaning Books:* cut one 7 3/4" piece.

CUT ONE 1 3/4" × 22" STRIP. FROM IT, CUT THE FOLLOWING:

☐ *For the Telephone:* cut one 3 1/2" piece.

CUT ONE 2" × 22" STRIP. FROM IT, CUT THE FOLLOWING:

☐ *For the Hobby Horse:* cut one 3 1/2" piece.

☐ *For the Building Blocks:* cut two 2 1/4" pieces.

CUT ONE 2 1/4" × 22" STRIP. FROM IT, CUT THE FOLLOWING:

☐ *For the Telephone:* cut two 2 1/4" pieces.

CUT ONE 2 1/2" × 22" STRIP. FROM IT, CUT THE FOLLOWING:

☐ *For the House:* cut one 4" piece.

☐ *For the Sailboat:* cut one 4 1/4" piece.

CUT ONE 3 1/2" × 22" STRIP. FROM IT, CUT THE FOLLOWING:

☐ *For the Telephone:* cut one 6" piece.

Green Fabric

☐ *For the Telephone:* cut two 1" squares.

☐ *For the Building Blocks:* cut one 2 1/4" square.

☐ *For the House:* cut one 2 1/2" × 6" piece.

Yellow Fabric

For faster cutting, fold the yellow fabric in half and cut these pieces through both layers.

☐ *For the Building Blocks:* cut two 2 1/4" squares

☐ *For the House:* cut two 1 3/4" squares.

☐ *For the Car:* cut two 1" × 1 1/4" pieces.

Blue Fabric

☐ *For the House:* cut three 1 1/2" × 2 3/4" pieces.

☐ *For the Building Blocks:* cut one 2 1/4" square.

White Fabric

☐ *For the Rocket:* cut one 3" × 6 1/4" piece.

☐ *For the Car:* cut two 1" × 1 1/4" pieces (headlights); cut two 1 1/4" × 3" pieces.

☐ *For the Doll:* using templates, cut one collar and one sleeve.

Skin-Toned Fabric

☐ *For the Clown:* cut one 1 5/8" square (hand); cut one 2 1/2" × 3" piece (face).

☐ *For the Doll:* using the templates, cut one face and one hand.

Cut the Miscellaneous Fabrics

To help you choose your miscellaneous fabrics, study the diagrams and photographs.

Miscellaneous Dinosaur Fabrics

☐ Cut one 1 3/4" × 6" piece (optional base).

☐ Cut one 1 3/4" × 2 3/4" piece (optional base).

☐ Cut four 1 3/4" squares (legs, tail).

☐ Cut one 1 3/4" × 2" piece (neck).

☐ Cut one 2" × 2 1/2" piece (head).

☐ Cut one 2 1/2" × 5 3/4" piece (body).

Miscellaneous Hobby Horse Fabrics

☐ Cut two 1 1/4" × 2" pieces (legs).

☐ Cut one 2 1/2" × 5" piece (body).

☐ Cut one 2 1/8" × 2 1/2" piece (head).

☐ Cut two circles (saddle; see page 73).

Miscellaneous Clown Fabrics

☐ Cut one 2" × 2 3/4" piece (shoe).

☐ Cut one 1 3/4" × 5 1/4" piece (clothes).

☐ Cut one 6 1/4" × 4 1/8" piece (clothes).

☐ Cut one 2 1/2" square (optional hat).

Miscellaneous Car Fabrics

☐ Cut one 1 1/4" × 2" piece (license plate; or cut it longer to fit your FLP's name).

☐ Cut one $1^{1}/2" \times 4^{1}/4"$ piece (grille).

☐ Cut two $1^{1}/4" \times 1^{1}/2"$ pieces (tires).

Other Miscellaneous Fabrics

☐ *For the Doll:* using the templates, cut one dress and one hat (see page 89).

☐ *For the Drum:* cut one $5^{1}/4" \times 5^{3}/4"$ piece.

☐ *For Betsy's Boat:* cut one $2^{1}/2" \times 8"$ piece.

☐ *For the Leaning Books:* cut one $1^{1}/2" \times 7"$ piece.

Finish Cutting Later

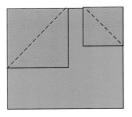

After you have made most of the Toy blocks and you and your FLP are arranging the blocks and making creative decisions, you'll still have some blocks to cut. That's the time to decide how big to make the Box block(s) and in what color(s). Look through the remnant box and your stash to find fabrics for the Standing Books and Leaning Books. Cut the books to any height and width and in any colors you need to balance the quilt top.

"ROUND OFF" THE RECTANGLES

The dotted-lines on the block patterns at the end of the chapter show where background squares will be used to "round off" the corners of rectangles or make large triangles. For the Dinosaur's tail and Clown's hat, other colors of fabric are used the same way.

Here's how these squares become triangles.

1 Line up the square and rectangle, referring to the block pattern to see which corners are being rounded off. Sew diagonally from one corner of the square to the other, as shown.

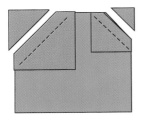

2 Trim off the surplus fabric, as shown. Then fold the triangle back and press the seam.

At her quilting retreat in Oregon, Anita shared early sketches for a Playroom Quilt with Laura Rohwedder, who went home to Pittsburgh, Pennsylvania, and made this quilt—without any further guidance—for her son Alex. It's quite different from Anita's version!

HOW TO ASSEMBLE AND EMBELLISH THE BLOCKS

When you have all the triangles pieced and main fabric pieces cut, stack your working papers very carefully to keep from losing any fabric, and move everything to the sewing machine. Piece together the blocks one or two at a time, following the assembly directions that follow. Remember, some embellishment will be done after the quilt is almost finished, because buttons and other trim would get in the way if you machine quilt your Playroom Quilt.

Be sure your FLP gets involved with the arrangement and embellishment of this quilt. If your FLP is very young and has a short attention span, do just one block a day. Efficiency isn't as important as enjoying each other's company. She can pass you pieces of fabric, clip threads, return sets to the working page, help with embellishments, and share the fun of seeing each block finished.

If you're doing the quilt by yourself, you'll probably find it easiest to chain piece and to make two blocks at a time. For example, sew background fabric to one side of the Drum, sew a rectangle to a Leaning Book, and sew a triangle to the second Leaning Book. Then clip them apart and sew a second piece to each set, and so on. The Box block and Standing Books blocks will be created later, after you've finished the rest of the blocks and are ready to start arranging your quilt.

DRUM

Assemble the parts of the drum as shown. You may want to add flat middy braid (or other trim) as you assemble the block, so the ends will be hidden in the seams.

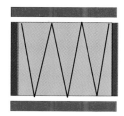

Do not add the background strips to the sides of Drum at this stage. When you arrange and assemble the quilt top, you can add the side strips to fill up space as needed.

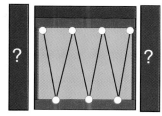

EMBELLISHMENT IDEAS
The diagrams show the placement of the braid, but don't worry about being too precise. Add buttons to the points of the trim, as shown.

LEANING BOOKS

Assemble the Leaning Book blocks as follows.

1 Cut rectangles for the books. Cut the left book 1¹/₄" × 7³/₄". Cut the right book 1¹/₂" × 7".

2 Add the extensions of the background color, as shown in the block pattern.

3 Sew together, offsetting the bottoms of the books by ¹/₂".

4 For the background, cut a 5" × 8" rectangle in half diagonally.

5 Sew the block together and trim the edges, as shown.

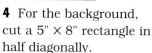

EMBELLISHMENT IDEAS
Add titles to the spines.

BUILDING BLOCKS

Assemble the blocks as shown.

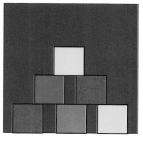

EMBELLISHMENT IDEAS
Use iron-on letters to make alphabet blocks.

BETSY'S BOAT

You should have cut off the ¹/₂" strip from one of the triangle sets earlier; if you didn't, do so now. Add the strip of background fabric between the sails, as shown.

Assemble the entire block as shown.

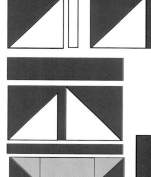

EMBELLISHMENT IDEAS
No embellishment is really needed for this block, but you could add a star, flag, number, or name if you wanted.

ROCKET

Assemble the block as shown. Add side strips in the background color of any size, as needed to fill out the shelf.

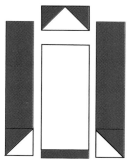

EMBELLISHMENT IDEAS
Use iron-on letters or numbers to identify the Rocket. Add an embroidered flag or star. Add a "seam" with stitching or fabric paint to the Rocket's body. Rivets can be made with small buttons, embroidery, or fabric paint.

HOUSE

Assemble the House as shown. You may need to trim off some of the background fabric along the left side, as shown. This block doesn't really need any embellishment.

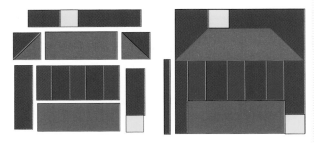

SAILBOAT

Assemble the block as shown. Although no embellishment is needed for this block, you may want to add a name to the boat.

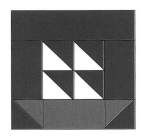

TELEPHONE

Assemble the Telephone block as follows.

Assemble the block as shown.

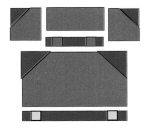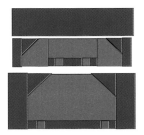

Trim the edges to even up the block.

EMBELLISHMENT IDEAS

Make a keypad by painting on squares or a dial by painting on circles. You could also use buttons. Arrange 10 buttons in a circle for a dial phone or 12 buttons in rows for a touch-tone phone. Embroider a circle or rectangle, as shown, if you wish.

DINOSAUR

Assemble the basic block as shown.

There are two ways to set the Dinosaur's tail. It can extend down into a "base," which is part of the block (see the photograph on page 73). Or the tail can extend down into the sashing, as shown in the Quilt Diagram. If you do this, add a strip of background fabric to the top of the Dinosaur block.

In either case, the tail is made as described in "'Round Off' the Rectangles," on page 70.

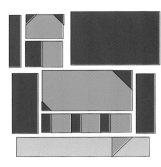

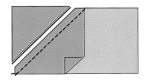

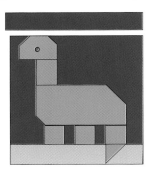

EMBELLISHMENT IDEAS

Use a button for the Dinosaur's eye. Add a leaf dangling from the Dinosaur's mouth.

CAR

Assemble the Car block as shown. You may want to add the steering wheel (a 3" piece of gold rattail cord or middy braid) when assembly the block, so you can hide the ends of the trim in the seams.

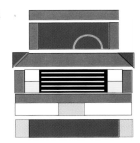

EMBELLISHMENT IDEAS

If you didn't use cord, you could embroider a steering wheel to show through the windshield. Personalize the license plate.

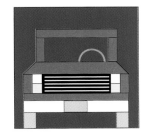

Another version of the
Playroom Quilt. Notice the Dinosaur set on a base.

HOBBY HORSE

The Hobby Horse can be assembled without the saddle and stirrup. Here's how to add the saddle during the block construction.

1 Draw two circles, about $2^1/2$" in diameter (just trace a fruit jar lid, perhaps) onto a piece of fabric that contrasts with the Hobby Horse's body. Modify the circles to get the saddle shape. Cut out.

2 Cut a 4" length of braid in any color you'd like. With right sides together and the ends of the braid in the seam, sew the curved edges of the saddle pieces together, as shown.

3 Clip the curved seam, turn the saddle right side out, and press.

4 Sew the straight edge of the saddle into the seam when assembling the block.

EMBELLISHMENT IDEAS

Stitch the saddle down with large stitches in a contrasting thread. Shape the stirrup and tack it down with hand stitching. Embroider a mane and tail or make them from yarn. Add a button for the eye.

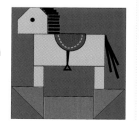

DOLL

The Doll block is assembled in several stages, but it really isn't difficult to do.

1 First piece the hat fabrics. Then use the template to trace the hat shape. Cut out.

2 Refer to the templates to see where the lace is attached. It is added as you construct the block so the raw edges can be hidden in the seams.

3 Assemble the block as shown.

EMBELLISHMENT IDEAS

Add a button or embroidered eye. Add yarn for the hair. Add a ribbon bow that matches the fabric used for the hat band in Step 1 or add flowers instead.

CLOWN

The Clown, as we mentioned earlier, is the most time-consuming block to embellish. Just take it one step at a time, and you'll end up with a terrific Clown for your Playroom Quilt.

1 First add the hat (if you want one) and the specially cut background square, as shown in the block diagram, in the same manner as described in "'Round Off' the Rectangles," on page 70.

2 Assemble the block as shown. You may want to add ruffles and rick-rack while you are assembling the block, so you can hide the raw edges in the seams. When you assemble the quilt, you can trim off $1/2$" along the right edge, making the Clown's foot a bit smaller.

EMBELLISHMENT IDEAS

Whether you decide to use the hat or not, the Clown will need a mass of yarn hair. Use buttons for the hat, for the nose, and on the clothes. Embroider or paint an eye and give the Clown a painted cheek.

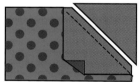

COMPLETE THE QUILT TOP

When all of the blocks described so far are pieced and pressed, square them up by trimming the edges off, if you haven't done so already. Don't worry if some blocks are taller than others, it probably doesn't matter, as we'll explain.

ARRANGE THE BLOCKS

Lay out blocks three, four, or five in a row, as shown in the Quilt Diagram and photographs in this chapter, or find another arrangement you and your FLP like. Keep the blocks that are a little too tall (or too short) together. Try to have the Hobby Horse and Dinosaur facing the center of the quilt top. Balance heavy and light blocks, and watch color placement. If a block just doesn't seem to fit, don't use it—make it into a pillow or potholder instead.

You can make the shelves shorter or longer than shown in the Quilt Diagram. Add more background fabric to the sides of any block to fill up space and make the blocks even. Plan where you will put the Standing Books and how many you'll make; leave empty spaces there.

Bookends give a feeling of stability, so try to flank Standing Book blocks with Toy blocks that look like they'd keep the books from tipping over. The Doll and Clown blocks are naturals. But you might also try one of the "heavy" blocks like the Dinosaur, Box, Drum, Leaning Books, or Horizontal Books.

CREATE THE LAST BLOCKS

Standing Book Blocks

If you have already cut out strips for the Standing Books, get them out now. Or go through your remnants and choose fabrics for the books. Cut strips from 1" to 2" wide and 5" to 7" long.

To make each book, just sew a large enough background piece to each book strip to make an 8" to 10" length. Trim off any extra width; the extra length is handy when sewing the blocks together. Even a young child can sew scraps together to make Standing Books.

ARRANGEMENT TIP
Place a wide Standing Book at one end of each row. That way you can easily trim all the rows to the same size after they're sewn up. You can introduce new fabrics when making the books, if you need them for color balance.

Sew enough strips together to fill each empty space, staggering the heights of the books randomly. You can use just 1 or 2 books or 15 to 20 books in a row. The more books you add, the better your quilt will look.

Press each block and trim off the top, bottom, and sides as needed.

Remember that you can also make Horizontal Books. Stack the books about 4" to 5" high. If they look more like board games, puzzles, or model kits, that's fine. Sew the background fabric above the stack to make the block as tall as the others.

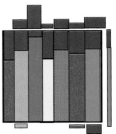

Be creative when you assemble the quilt top. For example, have some blocks sit on top of the bookcase. Or try making cubbyholes as shown here and in the photograph on page 70.

Box Blocks

For each Box block, cut a rectangle the size you need to fill in empty space. If you have a pretty metallic fabric, it might suggest a Treasure Box. If you have a cartoon print, it might be a Jack-in-the-Box. Other fabrics and sizes might be Games, Lunch Kits, Hat Boxes, or Pencil Boxes. To make a lid, sew a 1 1/2" strip of fabric in a coordinated color to the top of the box. Sew enough background fabric to the top to make the block 8" high. Add background fabric to the sides, as needed.

ASSEMBLE THE TOP

Sew the blocks together into rows. Consider sewing a strip of fabric a shade darker than the background color to the top of each row to give the illusion of depth to your shelves (this will make the quilt longer).

Measure the rows and cut sashing strips as needed, about 1 3/4" to 2" wide; the top and bottom strips can be wider. These pieces don't need to be made of the fabric you originally planned to use; changing your mind is part of what makes quiltmaking fun. Sashing strips that are a lighter shade of the background fabric are good, but design needs and the preferences of your FLP come first. Don't forget to add the tip of the Dinosaur's tail, if that's what you decided to do.

Sew the rows and sashing strips together. Add side borders in the same fabric as the sashing strips.

Add the outer borders. The sides and top might be made of fabric that suggests wallpaper, and the bottom border could then suggest carpet or flooring. You'll probably want to make the outer borders from 3" to 5" wide.

BORDER TIP

A narrow border of bright color in between the shelves and borders is nice. We're talking art now, so just please yourself and your FLP.

QUILTING AND FINISHING

Quilting the Playroom Quilt will be a creative challenge. If you haven't had much experience, have a friend or someone at your favorite quilt shop help you with a quilting strategy. See Chapter 2 for information about batting and preparing the project for machine quilting.

You might stitch the general outline of all the Toys, 1/4" from the edges, and do large-scale stippling in the background. For one Playroom Quilt we made, we quilted barely visible toy airplanes flying in the background and used stippling to suggest clouds. Don't do heavy background quilting because that would require more quilting within the toy shapes, and some Toy blocks look better without any quilting at all. When you have finished machine quilting your Playroom Quilt, see Chapter 2 for information about the binding. Add the final embellishments. For a quilt that will be used on a bed, make sure that everything is washable and fastened down thoroughly.

Make a Library Quilt

Make a twin-size quilt with five or six shelves of books. You really need only one or two Toy blocks (or Leaning Books) per shelf. You can make lots of books fast by strip-piecing them.

1 Join rectangles to a strip of background fabric.

2 Cut the panels into cross-sections that vary from 1" to 2 1/2" wide, as shown.

3 Mix up the colors and heights, and sew the pieces back together again. Trim the edges of the blocks, as shown.

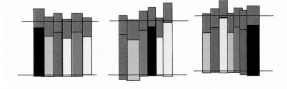

MORE IDEAS

Don't be afraid to design your own Toy blocks. Or try adapting one of the Pet blocks or Nine Patch Nature blocks from Chapter 6 to look like stuffed animals. How about making a mini-aquarium with a fish or two? Perhaps you could design a bird cage for one of the bird or butterfly blocks.

You may find that you can use squares of fabric that are printed with teddy bears or other toys. See Chapter 3 for how to use graphic prints.

Fill a whole quilt with multiple copies of the same Toy block. In Chapter 5, we gave you instructions for strip-piecing sets of Sailboats and Betsy's Boats. The Rocket blocks would be fast to make, since the small triangles can be strip-pieced and the rest of the block is simple. Look for a quick and inexpensive way to embellish them, such as using a printed fabric with flag motifs. If you make more than one copy of a Toy block, look for places to strip-piece: the legs and spaces of the Dinosaur and Hobby Horse blocks, the wheels and space in the Car block, and the windows and spaces of the House block are a few examples.

QUILTING SHORTCUT

Here's a quicker idea for quilting your project. Machine quilt the borders and around each Toy block. Then tie each block using your embellishments. Each button can be sewn through all layers of the quilt, as can some of the embroidery. Tie the book blocks with yarn or ribbon to suggest bookmarks. Try to place at least one tie or button in each block.

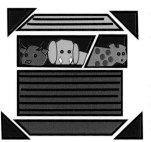

Embellish each block in a different way.

Here's how to make a Noah's Ark block. Cut a 3″ × 7″ (or so) piece of an animal print, one with a nice view of several animals. Cover any awkward parts in the print with one or two cutout animal heads appliquéd in place after most of the quilt top is assembled. The ark is simply a rectangle of fabric with horizontal lines. Round off the corners with squares of background fabric. See the photograph on page 70 for another version of a Noah's Ark.

Here's an easy way to make A-B-C blocks. Cut out squares of fabric with printed letters of the alphabet and build up borders of contrasting colors, as shown.

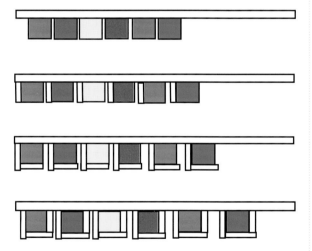

Cut the sets apart and assemble as shown.

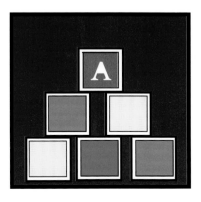

Make a reversible quilt. Make two of each block and put scattered blocks on the back. This doubles the time spent in piecing the quilt, and you'll need to use a lot of imagination, but it'll be a memorable quilt. Building Blocks that are stacked on the front can be either orderly or scattered on the back (orderly is quicker to make). Quilt the front with dark transparent thread, outlining the shapes, and don't worry about what happens on the back. Here's an example of how to piece the back.

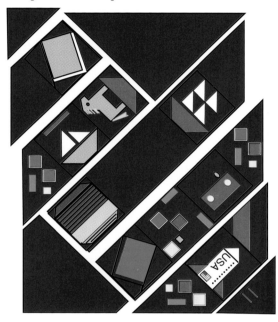

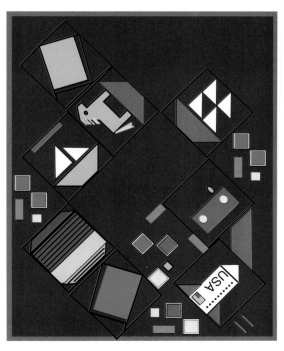

Have fun planning this project, but keep it simple enough that you can finish it before your Favorite Little Person is a teenager! ★

DRUM

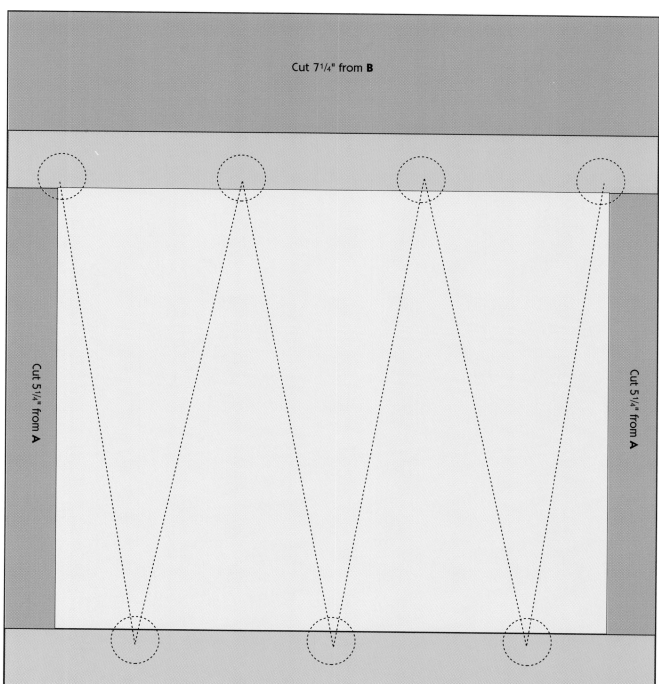

Cut 7¼" from **B**

Cut 8" from **A** (or make any width needed to fill up spcae)

Cut 5¼" from **A**

Cut 5¼" from **A**

LEANING BOOKS

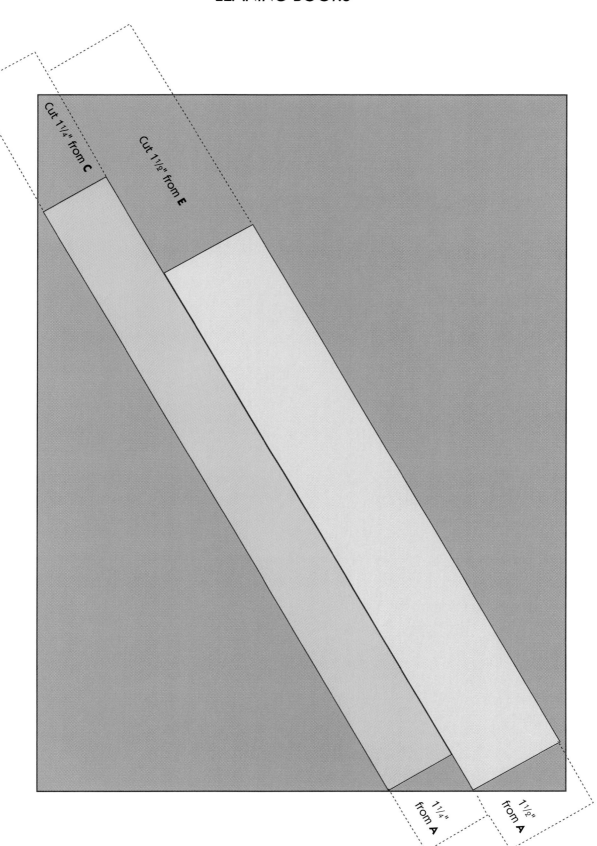

Cut 1¹/₄" from **C**

Cut 1¹/₂" from **E**

1¹/₄" from **A**

1¹/₂" from **A**

BUILDING BLOCKS

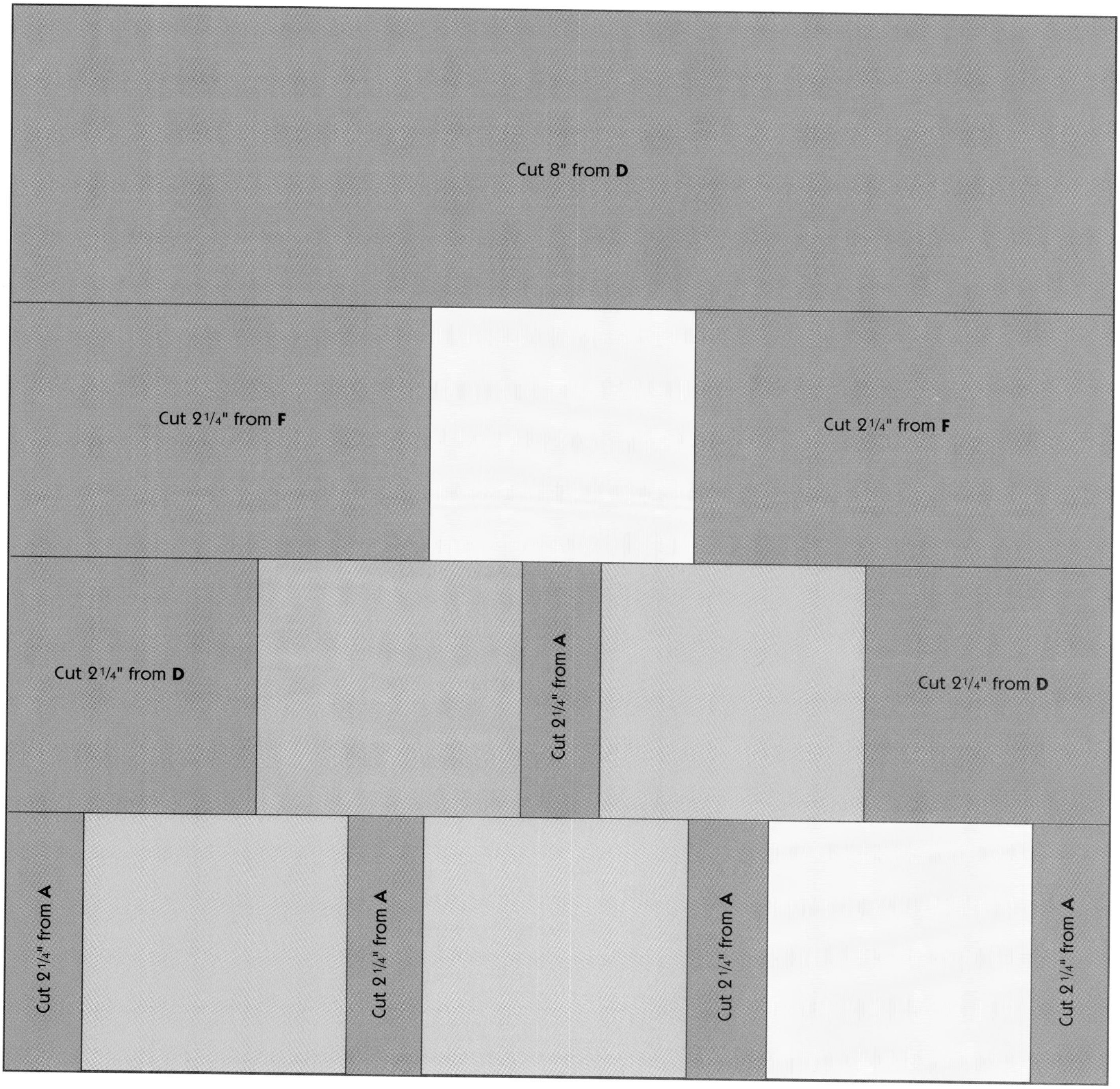

Cut 8" from **D**

Cut 2¼" from **F**

Cut 2¼" from **F**

Cut 2¼" from **D**

Cut 2¼" from **A**

Cut 2¼" from **D**

Cut 2¼" from **A**

Cut 2¼" from **A**

Cut 2¼" from **A**

Cut 2¼" from **A**

BETSY'S BOAT

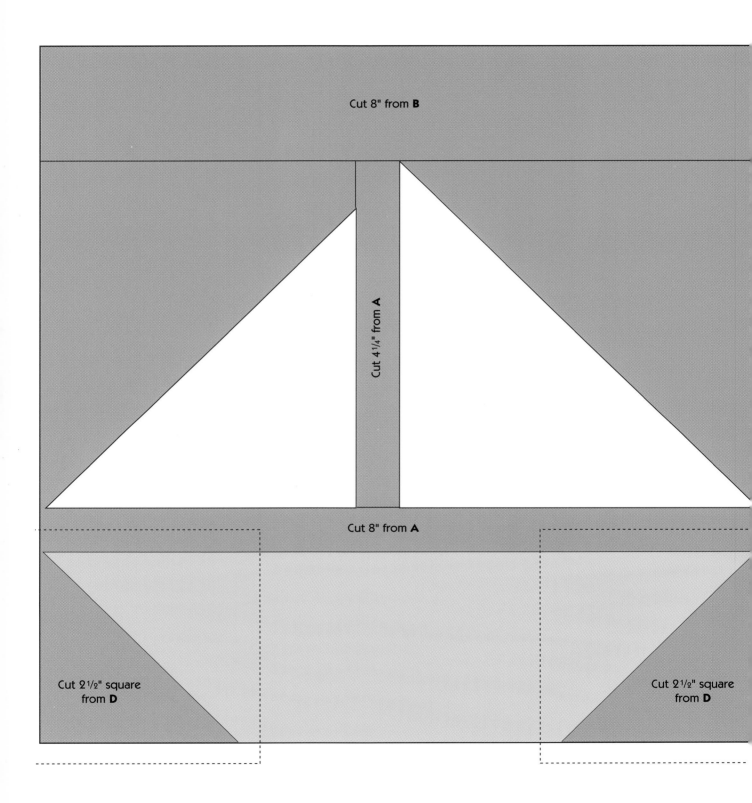

Cut 8" from **B**

Cut 4¼" from **A**

Cut 8" from **A**

Cut 2½" square from **D**

Cut 2½" square from **D**

ROCKET

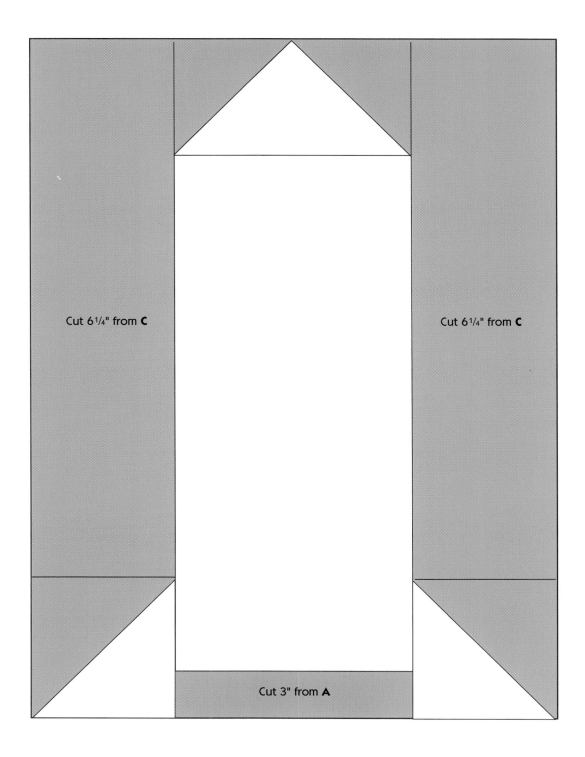

Cut 6¼" from **C**

Cut 6¼" from **C**

Cut 3" from **A**

HOUSE

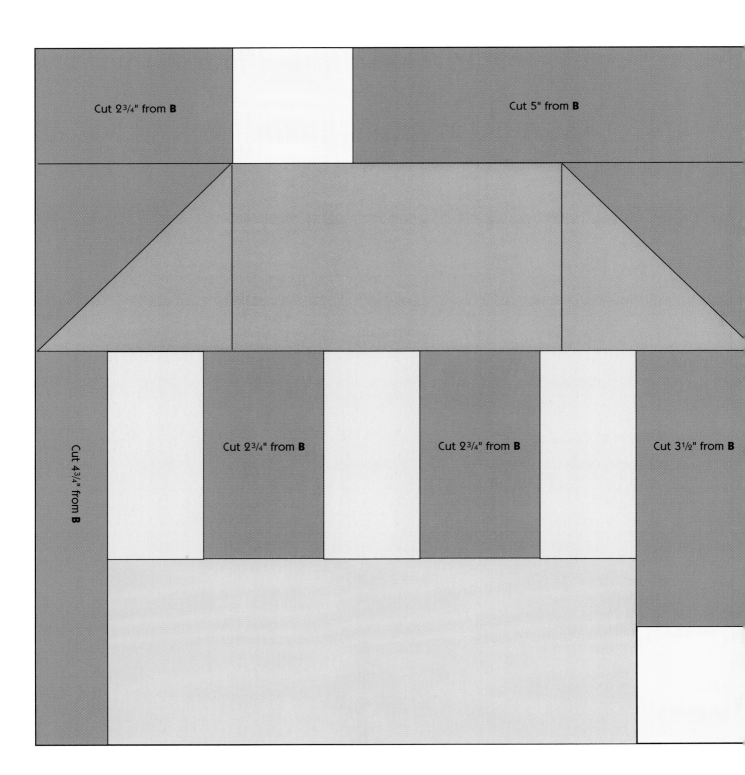

Cut 2³/₄" from **B**

Cut 5" from **B**

Cut 4³/₄" from **B**

Cut 2³/₄" from **B**

Cut 2³/₄" from **B**

Cut 3½" from **B**

SAILBOAT

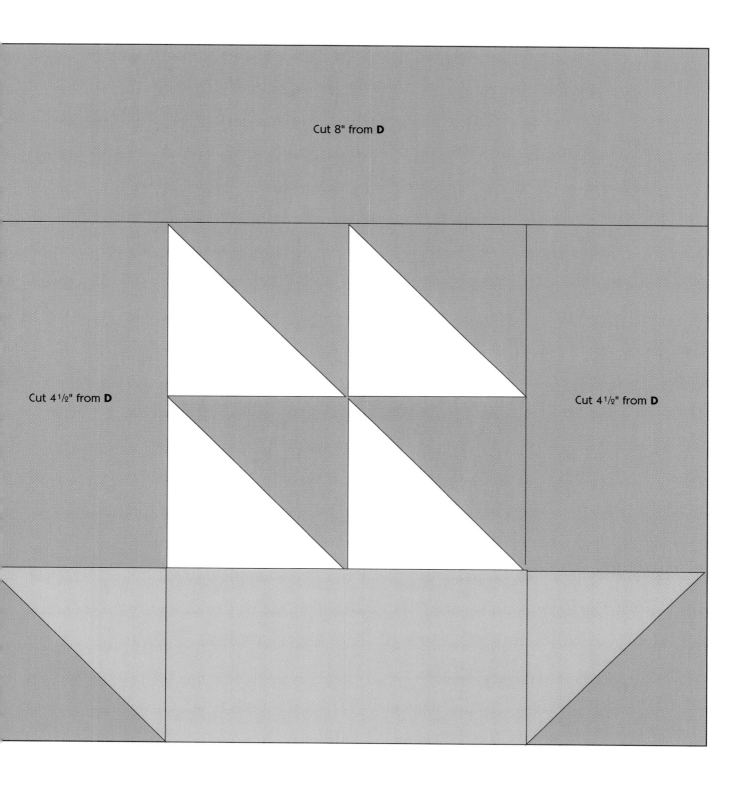

Cut 8" from **D**

Cut 4½" from **D**

Cut 4½" from **D**

TELEPHONE

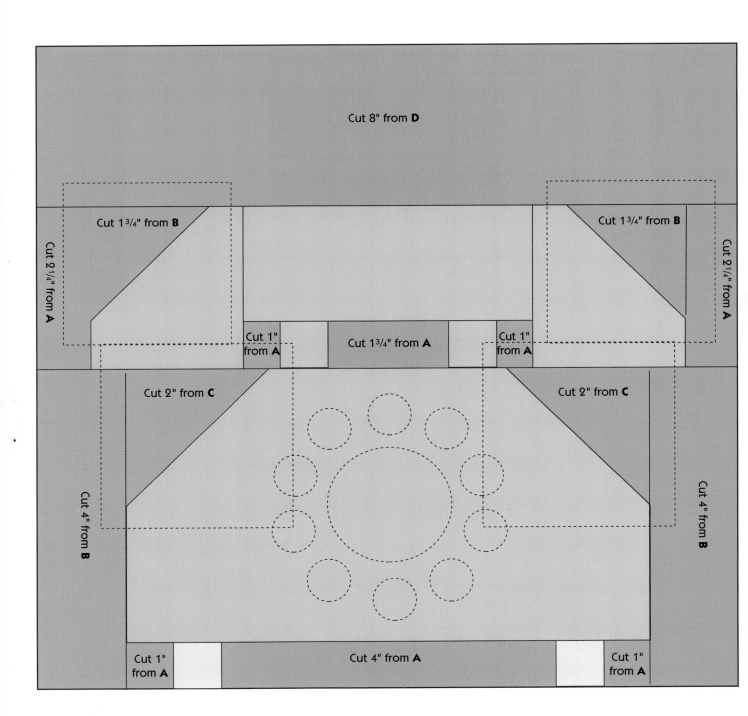

DINOSAUR

Cut 1" from **A**

Cut 1" from **A**

Cut 5½" from **F**

Cut 3½" from **A**

Cut 1¾" from **C**

Cut 1¾" from **B**

Cut 4" from **C**

Cut 4" from **B**

Cut 1" from **A**

Cut 1¾" from **A**

Cut 1¾" from **A**

Cut 1¾" from **A**

CAR

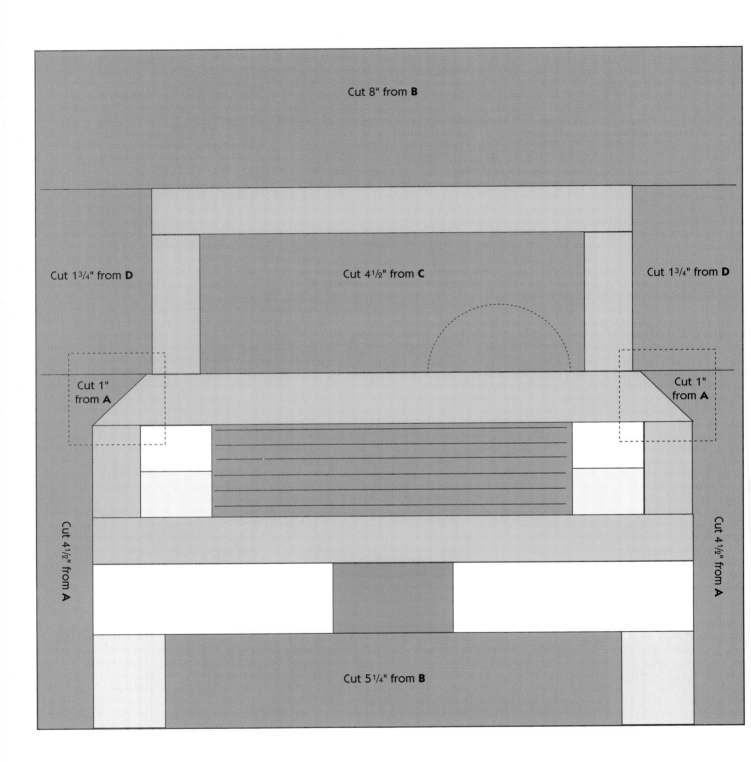

HOBBY HORSE

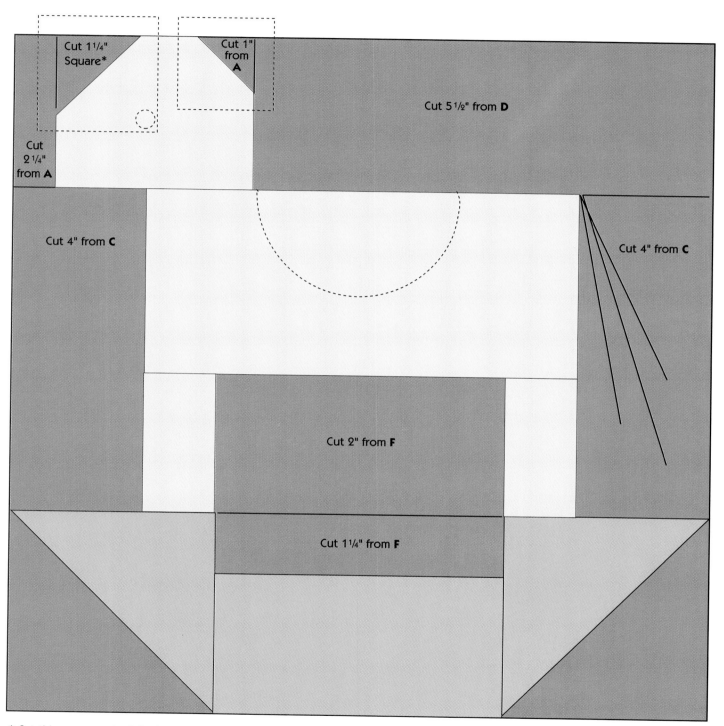

Cut 1¼"
Square*

Cut 1"
from
A

Cut 5½" from **D**

Cut
2¼"
from **A**

Cut 4" from **C**

Cut 4" from **C**

Cut 2" from **F**

Cut 1¼" from **F**

* Cut this square out of the background fabric.

DOLL

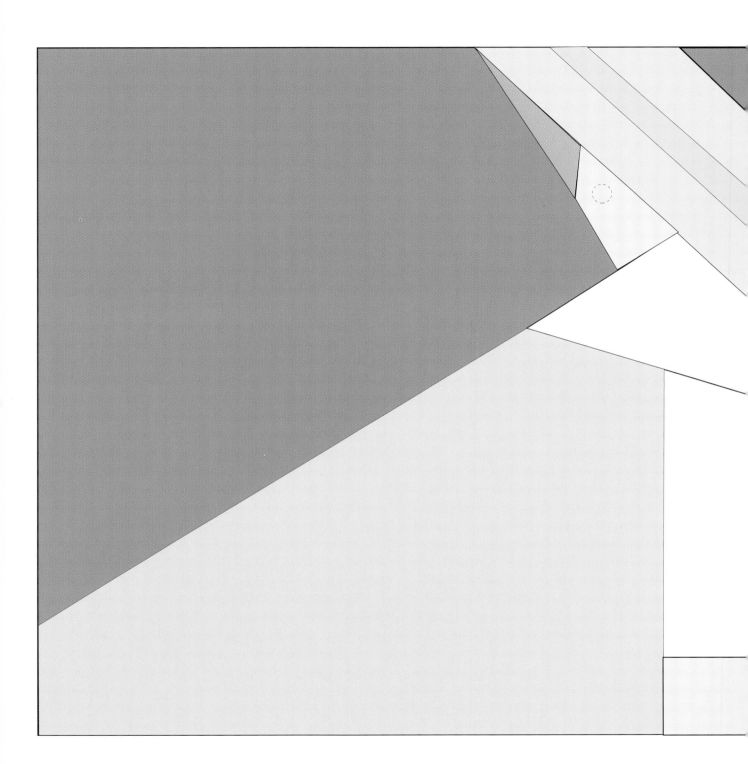

DOLL TEMPLATES

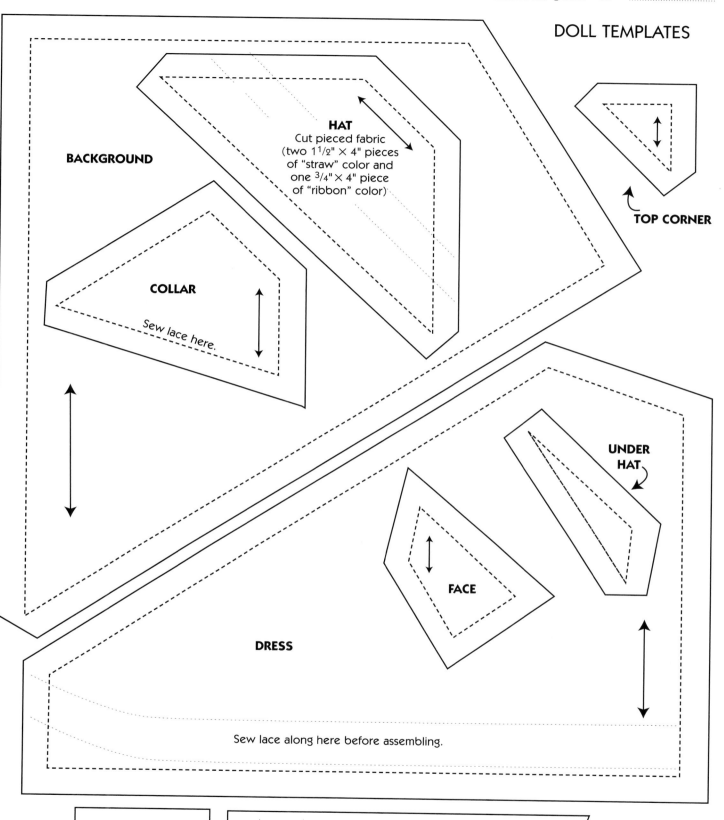

BACKGROUND

HAT
Cut pieced fabric
(two $1^{1}/_{2}$" $\times$ 4" pieces
of "straw" color and
one $^{3}/_{4}$" $\times$ 4" piece
of "ribbon" color)

TOP CORNER

COLLAR

Sew lace here.

UNDER HAT

FACE

DRESS

Sew lace along here before assembling.

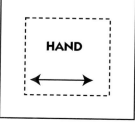

HAND

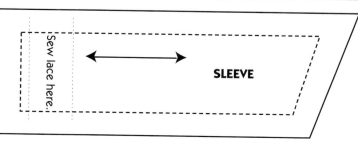

Sew lace here.

SLEEVE

CLOWN

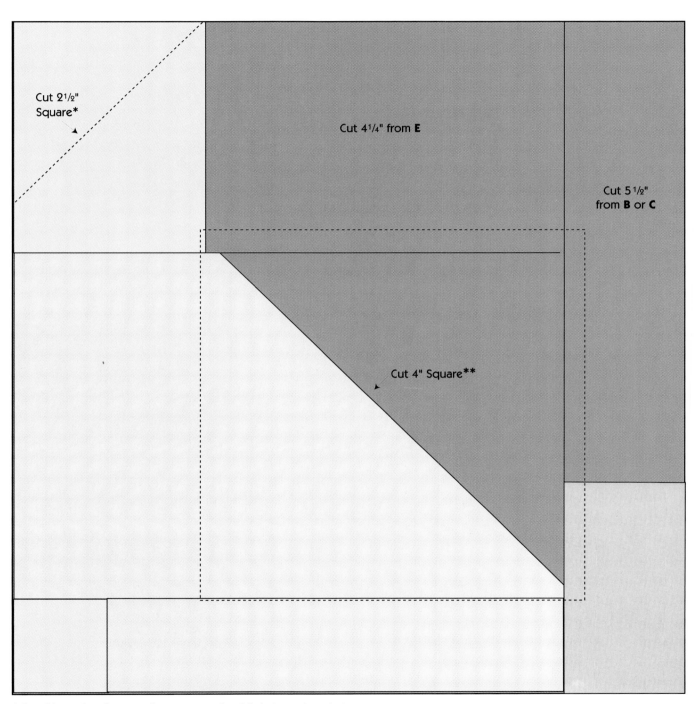

Cut 2½"
Square*

Cut 4¼" from **E**

Cut 5½"
from **B** or **C**

Cut 4" Square**

* Cut this optional square from contrasting fabric to make a hat.
** Cut this square from the background fabric.

Appendix

Here you will find instructions for making a Coordinated Nursery Set, templates for the Nine Patch Nature blocks, the Glossary, and "Special Things to Order."

I made this Flower Bed quilt in a cool color scheme.

A COORDINATED NURSERY SET

For an extra-special nursery, make a bumper pad, under-crib ruffle, and curtains to match your quilt. Betsy designed this set, since she's the one with a baby right now.

BUMPER PAD

This padded crib liner is approximately 11" wide for a crib with a mattress size of 26" × 52". The middle ribbons tie around the bars of the crib, and the end ribbons tie to each other, behind a corner post.

FABRIC

✦ 2¼ yards of a fabric to match your quilt. If you choose a border print, be sure it can be divided lengthwise into at least four sections. If using a fabric that wouldn't look good on its side or upside down, get 3¾ yards so you can be sure to get the best effect (you'll have a long section left over to use for other projects). For a reversible pad, buy 1¼ yards of two fabrics.

✦ 2¼ yards of 6 oz. or thicker batting, if 40" wide; 1½ yards, if 60" wide.

✦ 4³/₄ yard of bias tape for the top edge.

✦ 7¹/₂ yards of bias tape or ³/₈" ribbon for the ties.

MAKE THE BUMPER PAD

1 Cut the fabric in half the long way, making two 81"× 21" pieces.

2 Sew the pieces together end to end to make a 161"-long strip

3 Fold the strip lengthwise, wrong sides together, and press. This crease, which will be the bottom edge, is your guide for attaching the batting.

4 Cut and piece batting. Cut the batting into strips the same width as the fabric. If you're using a 40"-wide batting, cut four strips. If you're using a 60"-wide batting, cut three. Join the batting end to end with a wide zigzag stitch.

5 Sew the batting to the fabric.

a Lay the batting out on the wrong side of the fabric, center it, and check the measurements. The fabric should be 161" long (or at least 160"); the batting should be ¹/₂" shorter on each end. Pin the batting in several places with safety pins (avoiding the edges and center crease).

b Turn the pieces so the fabric side is up. Sew the layers together along all four edges and along the crease.

6 Cut all the ties and add the end ties.

a Cut the bias tape or ribbon into four 11" pieces and ten 21" pieces. If you're using bias tape, sew the edges closed first. If you're using ribbon, cut the ends at an angle and treat them with Fray Check to prevent raveling. Set the 21" ties aside.

b Tack the ends of two of the 11" ties to each end of the bumper pad, one 1¹/₂" from one edge, the other 1¹/₂" from the stitched center line, extending over the right side of the fabric with the ends even with the edge of the fabric.

7 Sew the ends of the Bumper Pad. Fold the pad over lengthwise, right sides together, and sew up the ends, making sure the free ends of the ties don't get caught in the seams. Place a piece of tissue paper or tear-away stabilizer over the batting to keep it from getting caught in your presser foot.

Remove the paper, and trim any extra batting to eliminate bulk.

8 Turn the Bumper Pad right side out. Even up the edges and pin them together. Machine baste the long edge, catching the batting in the seam. Trim the edges to ¹/₄" from the stitching.

9 Bind the edges with bias tape. Fold the raw ends under to create a nice finished end. Pin, then sew.

10 Sew creases and add the 21" ties. Divide the Bumper Pad into six even sections, each approximately 26¹/₂" long. Mark crosswise lines. Stitch along those lines to create the creases for folding the pad. As you sew, attach the 21" ties, 1¹/₂" down from the top and up from the bottom, by sewing through the center of each one. Secure by backstitching.

11 Add top stitching or light quilting if you wish, keeping the ribbons out of the way.

VARIATIONS

✦ **Add Ruffles.** Instead of using bias binding, use eyelet lace or ruffles along the top, covering the edge with single-fold bias tape sewn down along both edges.

✦ **Make a Reversible Pad.** Piece together two different lengths of fabric. Sew ties to both sides (tie the inside ones in bows when they aren't being used).

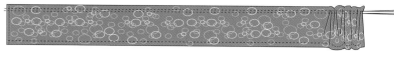

DUST RUFFLE FOR A CRIB

This dust ruffle goes between the mattress and springs, with the ruffle hanging down on each side.

FABRIC

✦ 27" × 51" piece of muslin or other fabric for the top, which won't show.

✦ 2 yards of fabric—the same as or to coordinated with—the Bumper Pad.

MAKE THE DUST RUFFLE

1 Cut the ruffle fabric into quarters lengthwise. The pieces will be 10" to 11" wide. Join them to make a piece 8 yards (288") long.

2 Cut the long piece into three sections. Two pieces will be used on the edges. Cut the other piece in half for the ends.

3 Hem the ends and one side of each long piece.

4 Gather the other long side to fit the large muslin rectangle, as shown.

5 Pin each piece of ruffle fabric in place along the edges of the muslin fabric. Sew with a wide enough seam to enclose the gathering stitches.

Hannah (age one) sits on a Grandma's Secret Quilt made by her mother, Betsy. The coordinating bumper pad and dust ruffle are on her crib. The quilt directions are given in Chapter 4.

TEMPLATES FOR MAKING NINE PATCH NATURE BLOCKS

Use the templates given here instead of strip-piecing the Nine Patch Nature blocks, if you prefer. There is one set of templates for the regular size blocks and one set for the smaller blocks.

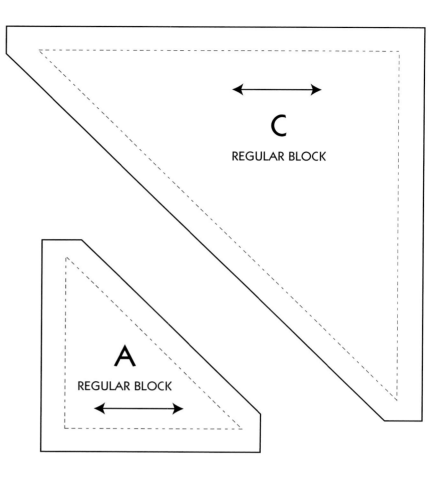

C
REGULAR BLOCK

A
REGULAR BLOCK

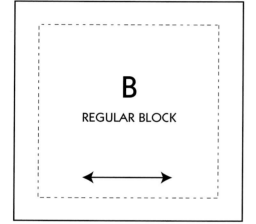

B
REGULAR BLOCK

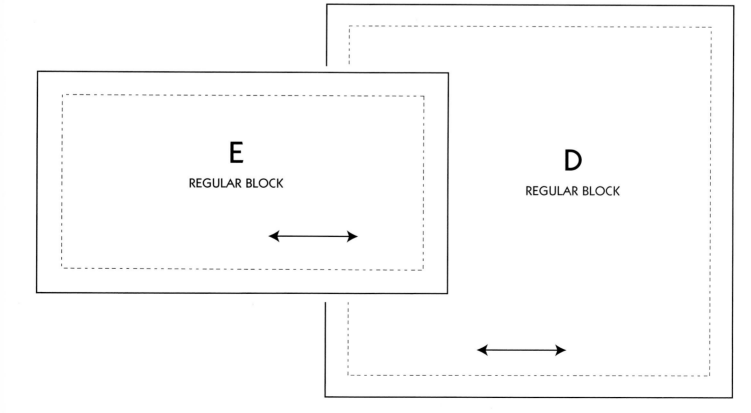

E
REGULAR BLOCK

D
REGULAR BLOCK

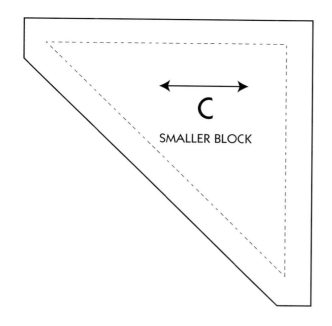

C

SMALLER BLOCK

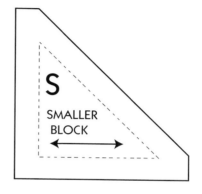

S

SMALLER
BLOCK

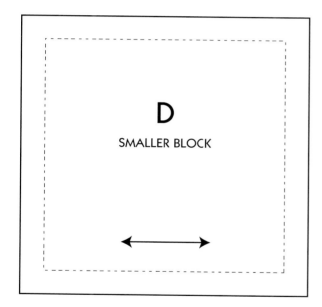

D

SMALLER BLOCK

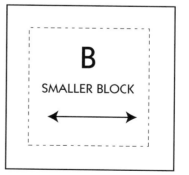

B

SMALLER BLOCK

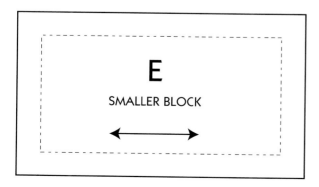

E

SMALLER BLOCK

SPECIAL THINGS TO ORDER

We have designed many more quilts and blocks than can be included in a single book. If you need special instructions, send $2 for copying, postage, and handling to Anita Hallock at Box 2, Springfield, OR 97477.

The following items are available.

✦ Chapter 3: yardage and step-by-step directions for all the quilts used to illustrate the block arrangement. (Please specify the diagram.)

✦ Directions for making the Dancing Squares border in David's quilt shown in the photograph on page 27.

✦ Flower basket appliqué pattern for Hannah's quilt shown in the photograph on page 60.

✦ Chapter 5: full-size drawing of the lighthouse (shown on page 45) to use for making templates.

✦ Shells and seaweed appliqué pattern in Betsy's Ocean Quilt shown in the photograph on page 7.

I made this quilt for my granddaughter Caitlyn. It is a Woodpile quilt from my book Scrap Quilts Using Fast Patch.

Glossary

Beta strip. Strip that matches the size of the strips of triangles, especially in the width (it is often in a longer length for convenience). It will become squares. It may also be used for rectangles and in sashing for many strip-pieced projects.

Chain. The final set of triangles, squares, and other shapes ready to be assembled into a block.

Chain-piecing or chaining. Stitching one seam after another without breaking the thread between pieces.

Checkerboard. Quilt block with alternating dark and light squares or a panel that will be turned on an angle and cut apart into strips of triangles with the Fast Patch method.

FLP. Favorite Little Person.

Panel. In strip-piecing, the stage at which strips are sewn together, ready to be cut into cross-sections. This is sometimes called "strata."

Quick-turn method. Way of sewing the quilt top and lining together; stitching around the edges and turning right side out so edges don't need to be bound.

Sashing. Small borders between and around blocks.

Sawtooth chain. A group of triangles all facing the same direction, ready to be assembled into a block such as Sawtooth Flower or Maple Leaf.

Two-Square method. An alternate Fast Patch method of strip-piecing triangles so the bias is in the traditional position.

Index

A

Angel Fish blocks, 56
Aquarium wallhanging, 63
Arrangement tip, 74

B

Baby quilts, 11
Backing, 11-12
Batting, 11
Bear's Paw blocks, 61
Bear's Paw Quilt, *63*
Beautiful Publications, 14
Beta strips, 38-39, 97
Betsy's Boats blocks, 40, 42-43, 65, 71, 80
Betsy's Boats quilt, *34, 42,* 40-45
Betsy's Ocean wallhanging, *7,* 62, 96
Big Foot, 14
Binding, traditional, 15
Block arrangements
    alternating plain blocks, 18
    arranging blocks for, 22
    finishing for, 22
    setting blocks on point, 20-22
    simple, 18-19
    Storybook quilt
        Checkerboard Storybook Quilt, 21, 23-24
        embellishment for, 21
        fabric for, 22
        general instructions for, 22
        Nine Patch Storybook Quilt, 21-23
        pictures for, 21
        Twin Storybook Quilt, 21, 24-25
    strip-piecing blocks for, 22
    versatility of, 17
Blocks for borders, 60
Book blocks
    leaning, 65, 71, 78
    standing, 65
Borders, quilt, 11, 59-60, 75
Box blocks, 65, 74
Broadcloth, 7
Building Block blocks, 65, 79
Bumper pad for nursery set, 91-92
Butterfly blocks, 48
Butterfly Fish blocks, 54
By the Lake wallhanging, 63

C

Car blocks, 66, 72, 86
Care tags, 2

Chain, 97

Chain, 97
Chaining, 97
Chain-piecing, 9, 97
Checkerboard block
    Dancing Squares Quilt, 32-33
    defined, 97
    Fast Patch method for, 34-36, 42-43, 97
    Flannel Scrap Quilt, 28
    Grandma's Secret quilt, 30-32
    Jiffy Quilt, 28-30
    sizes of quilts using, 26-27
    Checkerboard Storybook Quilt, 21, 23-24
    strip-piecing for, 10
    Two-Color Checkerboard Quilt, 27
Chino, 7
Claire Shaeffer's Fabric Sewing Guide, 6-7
Clown blocks, 66, 73, 90
Color
    choosing, 7-8
    cool, 8
    for Grandma's Secret quilt, 30
    of kids' quilts, 7-8
    thread, 6
    tips, 30
    in Triangle arrangement, 39
    warm, 8
Cotton fabrics, 6-7
Cotton thread, 6
Cotton-wrapped polyester thread, 6
Crochet cotton, 13
Cutting mat, 6
Cutting tips, 32

D

Dancing Squares arrangement
    Dancing Squares Quilt, *26,* 32-33
    in setting on point, 20
Denim, 7
Designs, easy, 3. *See also specific types*
Dinosaur blocks, 66, 72, 85
Dinosaur Quilt, *17*
Dittmar, Pam, 62, 63
Doll blocks, 65, 66, 73, 88
Double-knit polyester fabric, 7
Drum blocks, 65, 71, 77
Dust ruffle for crib, 93

E

Embellishment
    for Playroom Quilt, 66-67

for Storybook quilt, 21
tips, 71-73
in tying, 13
Embroidery floss, 13
Even-feed foot, 14

F

Fabric
backing, 11
batting, 11
for Betsy's Boats quilt, 40, 42
bleeding of, 7
for bumper pad, 91-92
for Checkerboard quilts
Flannel Scrap Quilt, 28
Grandma's Secret, 30
Jiffy Quilt, 29
Two-Color Checkerboard Quilt, 27
cutting strips of, 6
durable, 7
for dust ruffle, crib, 93
for kids' quilts, 2, 6-7
for Nature Blocks, Nine Patch
individual blocks, 36
quilt, 58
plaids, 8-9
for Playroom Quilt, 66-67
prewashing, 6-7
prints, 7-9
solids, 8-9
for Storybook quilts
Checkerboard Storybook Quilt, 23
Nine Patch Storybook Quilt, 22
strip-pieced blocks, 22
Twin Storybook Quilt, 24
stripes, 8-9
for wallhangings, 8
Fast Patch: A Treasury of Strip Quilt Projects
(Hallock), 34, 61
Fast Patch checkerboard method, 34-36,
42-43, 97
Fast Patch two-square method, 36-37, 97
Favorite Little Person (FLP), 1, 97
Finishing
edges, 15-16, 97
Storybook quilt, 22
Fish-in-a-Flash blocks, 57
Flannel, 7
Flannel Scrap Quilt, 28, *28*
Floss, 13
Flower Bed wallhanging, 62, *91*
FLP, 1, 97
Foisy, Nancy, 14
Four-block combination blocks, 61
Free-motion quilting, 6, 14

G

Gentle curves quilting, 14
Glossary, 97
Grandma's Secret quilt, *17*, 30-32

Grandmother's Choice blocks, 61
Group tying, 13

H

Hallock, Anita, 34, 61, 96
Hobby horse blocks, 66, 73, 87
House blocks, 65, 72, 82
Howell, Nona, 42

I

"It's Your Quilt" (Ridell), 3

J

Jiffy Quilt, *12, 29*, 28-30

K

Kamon, Chris, 46
Kids' quilts. *See also specific names*
assembling, 11-12
color of, 7-8
fabric for, 2, 6-7
finishing edges of, 15-16
involving kids in, 40
layering, 12
photographs of, 2
print fabric for, 7-9
quilting, 12-14
reasons for making, 1
tags for, 2
tying, 12-13

L

Layering quilt, 12
Leaves for sawtooth flowers, 59
Light/dark blocks, arranging, 39
Lining, quilt, 11

M

Machine quilting, 12-14, 22, 27-28, 30
Mail-order supplies, 14, 96
Maple leaf blocks, 51
Medallion quilts, 25, 62, *63*
Metallic thread, 6
Mini-Square Triangles, 37, 39

N

Nature Blocks, Nine Patch
Angel Fish blocks, 56
Butterfly blocks, 48
Butterfly Fish blocks, 54
cutting guide for, 47
fabric for
individual blocks, 36
quilt, 58
Fish-in-a-Flash blocks, 57

general instructions for, 47
Maple Leaf blocks, 51
number of blocks in, 47
organization for, 47
other creative ideas for, 61-63
quilt top for, 58
Sawtooth Flower blocks, 52
Simple Fish blocks, 55
Simplified Sawtooth Flower blocks, 53
Songbird blocks, 50
standard 15-block, 58-60
templates in, 47, 94-95
Tulip blocks, 49
wallhangings, 62-63
Needles, 6
Nine Patch blocks. *See also* Nature Blocks, Nine Patch
    setting blocks in, 19
    Storybook Quilt, 21-23
    strip-piecing, 10
Nine Patch Quilt, *17*
Nursery set, coordinated
    bumper pad, 91-92
    dust ruffle for crib, 93

O

One-person tying, 13

P

Panel, 97
Percale, 7
Pet blocks, 61
Photographs of quilts, 2
Picture block quilt, 40
Pictures for Storybook quilt, choosing, 21
Pieces, 6, 9, 97
Piecing. *See also* Strip-piecing
    Betsy's Boats quilt, 41
    chain, 9, 97
    Nature Blocks, Nine Patch, 57
        Angel Fish, 56
        Butterfly, 48
        Butterfly Fish, 54
        Maple Leaf, 51
        Sawtooth Flower, 52
        Simple Fish, 55
        Simplified Sawtooth Flower, 53
        Songbird, 50
        Tulip, 49
    speed method of, 30-31
    traditional vs. strip, 9-10
Pima cotton fabric, 7
Plaid fabric, 8-9
Playroom Quilt, *64, 70, 73*
    arranging blocks for, 64
    assembling, 70-73
    Betsy's Boats blocks, 65, 71, 80
    Box blocks, 65, 74
    Building Block blocks, 65, 79
    Car blocks, 66, 72, 86
    Clown blocks, 66, 73, 90

cutting fabric for, 67-70
    Dinosaur blocks, 66, 72, 85
    Doll blocks, 65-66, 73, 88
    doll template for, 89
    Drum blocks, 65, 71, 77
    embellishment for, 66-67
    fabric for, 66, 67
    finishing, 75
    Hobby Horse blocks, 66, 73, 87
    House blocks, 65, 72, 82
    Leaning Books blocks, 65, 71, 78
    organization for, 67
    other ideas for, 75-76
    overview of blocks, 65
    pieces for, 67
    quilt top for, 74-75
    Rocket blocks, 65, 71, 81
    rounding off rectangles for, 70
    Sailboat blocks, 66, 72, 83
    size of blocks for, 64
    Standing Books blocks, 65
    Telephone blocks, 66, 72, 84
    triangles for, 67-68
    working pages for, 67, 77-88
    work space for, 67
Polyester thread, 6
Poplin, 7
Presser feet, 14
Pressing, 9
Prewashing fabric, 6-7
Print fabric, 7-9

Q

Quick-turn method for finishing edges, 16, 97
Quilter's ruler, 6
Quilting
    free-motion, 6, 14
    gentle curves, 14
    hand, 12
    machine, 12-14, 22, 27-28, 30
    straight line, 14
    tip, 28
    tying vs., 12-13
Quilt in the ditch, 28
Quilt top
    for Betsy's Boats quilt, 40-42
    for Checkerboard quilts
        Flannel Scrap Quilt, 28
        Jiffy Quilt, 29-30
        Two-Color Checkerboard Quilt, 27
    finishing pieced, 11
    for Nature Quilt, 58
    for Playroom Quilt, 74-75
    for Storybook quilts
        Checkerboard Storybook Quilt, 23-24
        Nine Patch Storybook Quilt, 22-23
        Twin Storybook Quilt, 24-25

R

Rectangular checkerboard for triangles, turning, 35
Ribbon, 13

Ridell, Nancy, 3
Rocket blocks, 65, 71, 81
Rohwedder, Laura, 70
Rotary cutter, 5
Rotary cutting tools, 5-6
Ruler, 6

S

Sailboat blocks, 44, 66, 72, 83. *See also* Betsy's
    Boats block
Sashing, 18-19, 97
Sawtooth chain, 97
Sawtooth Flower blocks, 52
Sawtooth Flower quilts, *9*
Scrap Quilts Using Fast Patch (Hallock), 34
Seam width, 9
"Secret friend" tag, 2
Sequences, recognizing, 24
Setting blocks
    alternating with plain blocks, 18
    on point, 20-22, 59
    with sashing, 18-19
Sewing machine, 6
Sewing supplies, 6
Sewing techniques, 9
Sewing tips, 32
Signing name, 2, 16
Simple block arrangements, 18-19
Simple Fish blocks, 55
Simplified Sawtooth Flower blocks, 53
Sister's Choice blocks, 61
Sizing, 9
Slant of triangles, 39
Smiling patch, 3-4
Solid fabric, 8-9
Songbird blocks, 50
Spray-on fabric finish, 9
Spreading out quilt, 12-13, 17
Spring Garden wallhanging, *7*, 62
Square checkerboard for triangles,
    turning, 35
Stippling quilting, 14
Stitch length, 9
Storybook quilts
    arranging blocks for, 22
    Checkerboard Storybook Quilt, *18, 21,* 23-24
    embellishment for, 21
    fabric for, 22
    finishing, 22
    general instructions for, 22
    Nine Patch Storybook Quilt, 21-23
    pictures for, 21
    strip-piecing blocks for, 22
    Twin Storybook Quilt, 21, 24-25
Straight line quilting, 14
Strata, 97
Striped fabric, 8-9
Strip-piecing
    Checkerboard, 10
    Nine Patch blocks, 10
    Storybook quilt blocks, 22
    traditional piecing vs., 9-10

    in Triangle arrangement, 34
Strippy Quilt, 25
Supplies, 5-6, 96

T

Tags, 2
Tapico quilt, *46*
Telephone blocks, 66, 72, 84
Templates, 6, 47, 89, 94-95
Thread, 6
Thread catcher, 9
Tie-as-you-go, 13
Tightly woven fabric, 7
Transparent square grids, 6
Transparent thread, 6
Triangles
    in Betsy's Boats quilt, 40-45
    Fast Patch checkerboard method for, 34-36,
        42-43
    Fast Patch two-square method for, 36-37, 42-43
    mini-squares for just a few, 37, 39
    side and corner, 20
    strip-piecing, 34
    success with
        arranging light/dark blocks, 39
        clipping off masses of seams, 38
        cutting beta strips, 38-39
        designing color schemes, 39-40
        ignoring blunt points, 39
        marking centers for some blocks, 38
        noticing slant of triangles, 39
Tulip blocks, 49
Twill, 7
Twin Storybook Quilt, 21, 24-25
Two-Color Checkerboard Quilt, 27
Two-Square triangles, 36-37
Tying, 12-13

W

Walking foot, 14
Wallhangings
    fabric for, 8
    Nature Block, 62-63
    tags for, 2
Walner, Hari, 14
"What's-on-Hand" Quilt, 25

Y

Yardage for backing, 11
Yarn, 13

About the Authors

Anita Hallock made her first quilt as a summer project in high school home ec. She found that patiently piecing together hundreds of little pieces was monotonous, so she gave up quiltmaking while she went to college, taught art and English in high school, and began raising six children.

In about 1982 Anita discovered the rotary cutter and learned that quilters were strip-piecing simple designs with squares. When she found a way to strip-piece *triangles* (which offered vastly more design possibilities), she changed all her ideas about quiltmaking and joined the quilting craze that has swept the country during the last twenty years.

In the years that followed, Anita self-published a variety of Fast Patch books and a couple of videotapes. Her first book for Chilton was *Fast Patch: A Treasury of Strip Quilt Projects* in 1989, followed by *Scrap Quilts Using Fast Patch* in 1991. She also developed Foxy Blocks, an interesting method for using strips to weave quilt designs such as Tumbling Blocks. Each year she gives many lectures and classes on her techniques (especially in parts of the country where her grandchildren live). With help from her husband George and friend Nancy Foisy, she sponsors annual quiltmaking retreats on the Oregon Coast.

Betsy Hallock made her first quilts in junior high. She took her sewing machine to Brigham Young University, where she met and married David Heath, a Spanish teacher. Betsy and Dave love kids and don't believe in mothers working outside the home. They don't believe in going into debt either, so Betsy found that with her mom's speed-piecing methods, she could supplement Dave's income by making quilts to sell. With Kelly, David, and Joseph playing near her sewing machine for five years, she made hundreds of quilts to sell at craft shows.

When Hannah was born, Betsy gave up the craft shows. She and the kids still make quilts for gifts, for fun, and to help Grandma Hallock try out new ideas. Along with remodeling and decorating their 120-year-old house in Cheshire, Massachusetts, Betsy and Dave line up host families for foreign exchange students.